A Taste of
At Table with Brunetti

WITHDRAWN FROM STOCK

A Taste of Venice:
At Table with Brunetti

Culinary stories by Donna Leon

Recipes by Roberta Pianaro

Illustrated by Tatjana Hauptmann

WILLIAM HEINEMANN: LONDON

Published by William Heinemann 2010

2 4 6 8 10 9 7 5 3 1

Text copyright © Roberta Pianaro/Donna Leon and Diogenes Verlag AG Zürich 2009

Recipes: English translation copyright © Janet Edsforth Stone 2009

Illustrations copyright © Tatjana Hauptmann and Diogenes Verlag AG Zürich 2009

Roberta Pianaro and Donna Leon have asserted their right under the Copyright, Designs
and Patents Act, 1988, to be identified as the authors of this work

First published in Great Britain in 2010 by
William Heinemann
Random House, 20 Vauxhall Bridge Road,
London SW1V 2SA

www.rbooks.co.uk

Addresses for companies within The Random House Group Limited can be found at:
www.randomhouse.co.uk/offices.htm

References to Donna Leon's books are to the UK paperback editions. In the United States,
two of the books are published with different titles. *The Anonymous Venetian* in Britain is
Dressed for Death in the US; and *A Venetian Reckoning* is *Death and Judgment*.

The Random House Group Limited Reg. No. 954009

A CIP catalogue record for this book
is available from the British Library

ISBN 9780434020195

The Random House Group Limited supports The Forest Stewardship
Council (FSC), the leading international forest certification organisation. All our
titles that are printed on Greenpeace approved FSC certified paper carry the FSC logo.
Our paper procurement policy can be found at: www.rbooks.co.uk/environment

Typeset by SX Composing DTP, Rayleigh, Essex
Printed and bound in Great Britain by
Butler Tanner & Dennis

*Asterisk in the extracts taken from the Brunetti novels indicates that there is a recipe available for these dishes – refer to the index at the end of the book, or to the detailed table of contents at the beginning of each section.

CONTENTS

Brunetti *a tavola*

It was never my intention to write a cookbook. After the publication of the fourth Brunetti novel, however, readers began to comment about what they viewed as the conspicuous presence of food and meals in the books. The Brunetti family, sometimes Brunetti alone or in the company of colleagues or friends, ate meals that struck many readers as exceptional in their quality, complexity, and sheer length.

At first, this response surprised me, for there had been nothing intentional, nothing precious, about the placement of meals in the books: these novels dealt to a certain degree with family life in Venice, and this was the way that I had, during the last forty years, observed Venetians to eat. Soon it became apparent that such comments came most often, one could say almost exclusively, from readers in countries – how to say this gracefully? – with a culinary culture different from the Italian? (Yes, that sounds sufficiently polite.) Though many Italians have read the books and remarked on them to me over the years, none has ever mentioned the presence of food: for them, as for me, Brunetti's meals are simply a part of the received culture. How else would people be expected to eat?

Certainly, all Venetians, all Italians, do not eat like this all of the time. But I think it is true to say that most of them were raised eating in this manner, and that they still see these long, sensual meals as the normal way to deal with food. It's not only Venetians who view food in this way: we non-Italians who live here, at least if we live here for any length of time, soon come to regard eating well as a normal part of daily life, worthy of attention but hardly of comment.

There is a refreshing lack of self-importance in the way Italians in general think and talk about food: it does not occur to them that their appreciation of food or their interest in it makes them in any way special. This is as normal to them as it is for the British to discuss the weather or for Americans to talk about money. Eating well is not an achievement, a cause for self-promotion and pride: it's simply something you do twice a day in a manner that will provide as much physical pleasure as possible.

One of the first things that was said to me when I came to Italy forty years ago, speaking not a word of the language, was '*Mangia, mangia, ti fa bene.*' Eat, eat, it's good for you. At first sound, the command seems to fit into clichéd ideas about Italians: one pictures a heavy-bosomed mother saying it to her numerous children, or the grandmother in some cloying pasta commercial gathering her family under the protective wings of her pappardelle. But, as I was soon to learn, this is nothing more than their recognition of a simple truth: eating is good for you, and eating well is better for you than eating badly. Further, the person who concerns him or herself with feeding you is often doing so out of a desire to keep you well or make you better. In short, it is a manifestation of love, the most simple – if you will, the most primitive – manifestation of love of which we are capable.

In the decades I've been in Venice, the person who has made that love most manifest is my best, oldest, and dearest friend here, Roberta Pianaro, known to all of us who love her as Biba. It was she and her husband Franco who first opened up this world of food as culture and food as love to me. I've been eating at their table and helping in their kitchen for more than thirty years, during which time they have taught me to open not only my mouth and my sense of taste to food, but my mind to it as well.

I don't know how to write a cookbook. I do, however, know how to write about my own experiences with food and cooking and cooks, always seen from the point of view of a person raised in one of those cultures I still don't know how to describe politely: best perhaps simply to call it a culture with a different attitude to food. After all, with two Irish grandmothers, one grandfather Spanish and the other German, I can hardly present myself as legitimate heir to a rich culinary tradition.

Italian life is filled with food: people talk about it constantly, spend a great deal of time shopping for it and preparing it, and devote a joyous amount of time to eating it. One has but to pay close attention to them when they talk about food, or when they cook and eat, to begin to understand how fundamental it is to the living of a happy life and how vital it is to Italian culture.

It is the great privilege of my life to have been absorbed, if not into Italy itself, then at least into one Venetian family. Roberta and Franco have, over the years, allowed me to become part of their lives, not only as a guest at their table but as a member, however much a latecomer, of each of their families.

When the idea of writing a Brunetti cookbook was first proposed to me I responded in the normal Italian fashion, by turning to my family for help. Whatever I've learned about food or how to prepare it I've learned during my years spent watching Biba in the kitchen, often sitting at the table and chopping vegetables or asking why something was done in a particular way or in a particular sequence. Though she learned some of the dishes she prepares from cookbooks, most of Biba's skill stems from being raised within a family that loved to cook and eat, and from having the good fortune to have been born with the culinary equivalent of perfect pitch. Often, when I asked why a certain spice had to be added to a particular dish, Biba could come no closer to an explanation than to say, 'Because it's best.'

I would not, and could not, have undertaken this project without her help. Each time we emerged from the kitchen, whether to test and taste what we had made or to share it with friends and the people we love, I was made aware of that fundamental truth that is the animating spirit of Italian cooking: *'Mangia, mangia, ti fa bene.'*

Strada Nuova

One of the most common subjects of lamentation in Venice – or just about anywhere, I suppose – is the refusal of the present to be as good as the past. Here, this failure is evident in many ways: too many tourists, too few Venetians, unaffordable rents, unresponsive politicians. These changes have followed upon more profound transformations in the purpose and function of the city. In recent times, Venice, like most cities, provided life and livelihood for its citizens, sometimes to as many as 150,000 of them. Today, instead, its primary purpose is to offer services to tourists – twenty million last year – and this in turn provides an increasingly precarious future to the remaining 50,000 Venetians.

One way to feel the truth of this in the pit of your stomach is to take a walk down Strada Nuova, the commercial centre of the Sestiere di Cannaregio, as solid and middle-class a section of the city as one could ever hope to find. Here the shops reveal what this change in purpose has done to the fabric of the city. I started buying food in these shops decades ago, when I first came to Venice as a tourist and then, as years passed, as a guest of the family of my friend Roberta, and then as a guest of her and her husband Franco. When I moved to Cannaregio in 1981, I continued to shop in the places where they shopped. The stores on Strada Nuova were numerous and provided just about any food a person could need, and they were closer to my home than the Rialto Market, visible on the other side of the Grand Canal.

More than twenty-five years later, Strada Nuova has changed in both appearance and function, and where we used to buy stracchino of the best quality, fresh pasta, or new cooking pots, there are now shops selling glass, glass, or – yes – glass. Let me take you by the hand and, like one of the perpetually lamenting women of the city, walk you along Strada Nuova and show you what tourism has done to us.

There on the right, just beyond Campo Santi Apostoli, there remains, thank heaven, Bisiol, selling chicken and meat for half a century, the majestic owner still sitting behind her cash register on the left. Not very far along was once Plip, the cheese shop, with that tall man who always wore his white hat while serving customers. People raved about his stracchino, and I remember eating it draped over polenta or using a crust of bread to scrape the last, almost-liquid bits of it from the wrapping paper so as not to let something so divine go to waste. He also had that wonderful Montasio his friend in the mountains produced, and who has found Montasio as good as that since he closed? He's gone now, replaced by an estate agency. My notary told me that, last year, 25 per cent of the house sales he handled involved foreigners who did not plan to live permanently in the city.

A bit farther along was the barber, but now they sell masks there. Up near Calle delle Vele, the *latteria* is gone, but since it was bought by Benevento to expand the store that sells sweaters and cloth, it has at least continued to sell things useful to residents. Continue past the opening of the *calle* and you'll see that Bellinato, the hardware store that served all of Cannaregio and where you could find anything, is gone, replaced by McDonald's. The butcher has also vanished but you can buy a cheap glass necklace there, and the store beside it that sold kitchen pots is now Benetton.

Then there is Campiello Testori, once the site of the trattoria with the enormous grapevine at the front. Families went there on hot summer nights, taking along their own dinners. Perhaps they'd order a half-litre of wine, buy *gassata* as a treat for the kids, and spend the evening talking to friends at the other tables. Now it's an Irish pub with loud music or soccer games on the giant television. The grapevine's gone; so are the kids. So too is the open-air fish stall that stood in the same *campiello*. The *calli* leading back towards the *laguna* from it were once filled with shops offering life-giving food: a *salumaio*, the *pasticceria*, the butcher, two fruit vendors. Most are boarded up now, though the former butcher shop now sells woven articles from the Middle East.

Continuing towards the bridge, you'll see that the florist is gone, replaced – after a brief period when it was a room full of public telephones – by masks, and the other fruit dealer is now a soap store whose acid fumes contaminate the entire area.

Turn around at the Ponte di S. Felice and head back towards Santi Apostoli, and you'll see that Borini, which had a broad selection of good wines and *liquori*, now sells inexpensive clothing for adolescent women of all ages. Cross Calle Ca' d'Oro: the Colussi shop that sold biscuits has been replaced by sporty clothing.

The other fresh fish stall at the front of Campo Santa Sofia is gone; so's the post office, which is now part of the luxury hotel that stretches all the way back to the Grand Canal, with another hotel just across the *campo*.

The shop that once sold fresh pasta now sells glass, and so do the two beside it. The Brasilia bar remains and so does the restaurant, though it once had a brief period of being Chinese. The florist is no more and the fruit dealer at the foot of the bridge now sells cheap plastic toys. And then you're back at the church.

Certainly, it is still possible to buy food along this part of Strada Nuova: no one starves to death in Venice. But when you come out of Il Fornaio with your fresh-baked bread, you are greeted by the smell coming from McDonald's.

Luckily, though, not far off is still the *traghetto* which, for half a Euro, will take you across to the Rialto Market, one of the abiding glories of the city, where the past remains and the all-encircling splendour of food seems without end.

Antipasti · *Antipasti*

In ancient times, *cicheti* – delicious, mouth-watering appetizers, or antipasti – were an established custom in the city of Venice, and today they are more popular than ever. If you walk into a bar you'll see on the counter a seemingly endless variety of dishes, large and small, overflowing with all sorts of delicious titbits.

Every bar has its specialities, and you often have to make several stops before finding your favourite. Octopus, marinated sardines, whelks, crabs, mantis shrimps, small meatballs, spleen, boiled beef salad, parsley potatoes, white beans, omelettes, artichokes and snails can all be found at the Rialto market – plus, of course, the imaginative person preparing them. In other words, an infinite combination of foods, to be washed down with a few *ombra* of white or red wine. Though if you've made the mistake of sampling a few of these delights before heading home and continuing with a good lunch, you'll often find you're already full and a bit tipsy . . .!

At home, when we invite someone over for lunch or dinner, we always prepare an antipasto to put the person at ease and whet that famous Italian appetite. We can make simple antipasti, like canapés or little sandwiches, or venture into something more sophisticated – still easy to make and, most importantly, good to eat.

Roberta Pianaro

ANTIPASTI
Antipasti

Savoury corn fritters   23
Fritelle gustose al mais

Chickpea balls   24
Palline di ceci

Canapé squares with aubergine   25
Crostoni alle melanzane

Baked omelette with courgettes   26
Frittata al forno con zucchine

Snails   27
Bovoletti

Seafood antipasto   28
Antipasto di mare

Shrimp, melon and rocket   31
Gamberetti, melone e rucola

Cuttlefish eggs   32
Latticini di seppia

Marinated sardines   36
Sardine in saor

Squid salad   38
Insalata di calamari

Fagottini with shrimps   39
Fagottini agli scampi

SAVOURY CORN FRITTERS
Fritelle gustose al mais

Serves 4

1 small red pepper, finely chopped

140g (4¾oz) tinned sweetcorn, drained

140g (4¾oz) cooked ham, finely chopped

2 medium eggs

4 tablespoons milk

a pinch of salt

a pinch of strong paprika

120g (4oz) flour

2 tablespoons extra virgin olive oil

lots of vegetable oil for frying

Put the red pepper, sweetcorn and ham into a bowl and set aside. In a second bowl, beat the eggs with the milk, salt and paprika. Add the flour and olive oil, blending to form a smooth, lump-free batter. Add the pepper, ham and corn, and mix again. Heat the vegetable oil in a high-sided pan or a deep-fat fryer. When ready, pour in spoonfuls of the mixture, two or three at a time. The little fritters will be cooked in no time. Once these are cooked, place gently on absorbent paper to drain. Serve at once.

Chickpea Balls
Palline di ceci

Serves 4
250g (9oz) tinned chickpeas, drained
1 sprig of fresh parsley, finely chopped
1 medium egg
a pinch of salt and freshly ground black pepper
1 garlic clove, crushed
4 tablespoons breadcrumbs
1 teaspoon baking powder
1 tablespoon extra virgin olive oil
lots of vegetable oil for frying

Crush the chickpeas in a mixing bowl with the parsley. Add the egg, salt, pepper, garlic, breadcrumbs, baking powder and olive oil and mix together to obtain a smooth, compact dough. With slightly dampened fingertips, form the mixture into balls the size of a walnut. Heat the vegetable oil in a high-sided pan or a deep-fat fryer. When the oil is hot, gently drop in the chickpea balls, a few at a time. Cook until golden brown, then drain on absorbent paper. Serve hot.

CANAPÉ SQUARES WITH AUBERGINE
Crostoni alle melanzane

Serves 4
8 square slices of bread, with crusts removed
8 slices of aubergine, grilled
400g (14oz) tinned tomatoes, drained of juice
130g (4½ oz) mozzarella cheese
a pinch of salt
a pinch of dried oregano
extra virgin olive oil

On each piece of bread place a slice of aubergine, then a piece of tomato, a slice of mozzarella, a sprinkle of salt and oregano, and a drizzle of olive oil. Line a roasting tray with foil, arrange the slices alongside each other, and place in a hot oven. They will be ready when the bread is toasted, so keep watching them and adjust the oven temperature if necessary.

BAKED OMELETTE WITH COURGETTES
Frittata al forno con zucchine

Serves 4

8 tablespoons extra virgin olive oil
800g (1¾lb) courgettes, sliced into discs 0.5cm (¼ inch)
50g (2oz) shallots, finely chopped
salt and freshly ground black pepper
a pinch of finely chopped fresh parsley
8 medium eggs
10g (¼oz) butter
100g (3¼oz) Emmenthal cheese, diced

Heat 7 tablespoons of the olive oil in a non-stick pan and add the courgettes, shallots, a pinch of salt and 2 tablespoons of water. Cook, stirring frequently, and add the parsley when the courgettes are nearly tender. Continue to cook until the water has evaporated (usually after about 20 minutes), leaving only the oil at the bottom of the pan. Break the eggs into a bowl and add a pinch of salt and pepper and the remaining 1 tablespoon of olive oil. Beat the mixture gently with a fork. Drain off the oil and then place the courgettes carefully in a buttered ovenproof dish, cover with the cheese and top with the beaten eggs. Put the dish into the oven and cook at a high temperature for around another 20 minutes. The omelette will be ready when it is puffed up all over. Serve at once, since it will quickly subside.

SNAILS
Bovoletti

Serves 4
800g (1¾lb) snails
salt and freshly ground black pepper
1 garlic clove, finely chopped
10 tablespoons extra virgin olive oil
a handful of fresh parsley, finely chopped

Wash the bovoletti snails, put them into a large pan and cover with lots of cold water. Place over a very low heat, watching to ensure that the snails emerge slowly from their shells, then turn the heat up to maximum. Once the water starts to boil, add a handful of fine salt, wait for the water to come to a full boil, then drain. When the snails have cooled, put them into a bowl and add the garlic, oil, parsley and a pinch of salt and pepper, mixing well. Taste and adjust the seasoning with salt, pepper and oil, if necessary.

Seafood Antipasto
Antipasto di mare

Serves 4

4 octopuses, each around 100g (3½oz)
8 mantis shrimps
16 large prawns
4 fresh or frozen scallops
5 tablespoons extra virgin olive oil
1 garlic clove, halved
salt and freshly ground black pepper
1 sprig of fresh parsley, finely chopped
3 tablespoons dry white wine
lemon (optional)

Remove from the octopuses the sac containing the entrails, as well as the mouth and the eyes. Wash the octopuses thoroughly, then put them slowly into a pan of boiling salted water, heads down, so that the tentacles curl up. Cover and cook over moderate heat for about 20 minutes. Remove the pan from the heat, add a bit of cold water to save them from overcooking and set aside for 15 minutes, then drain and cut them into four lengthways.

Wash the mantis shrimps and prawns and plunge them into a pan of boiling salted water. Once the water comes back to the boil, turn off the heat, drain the contents and leave to cool. Cut the mantis shrimps with kitchen shears along the length of the shell, tail included. Remove gently so as not to break them, leaving each head intact and attached to the body. Shell the prawns as well, removing the dark thread along the back. Open the scallops with a sharp paring knife, detach the nut and the coral, and remove the dark threads. Wash the scallops very carefully, including the four hollow shells, and dry with kitchen paper.

Put the olive oil, garlic and a pinch of salt into a non-stick frying pan and brown without burning. Remove from the heat and discard the garlic, then add the scallops, a pinch of parsley, the wine and a grinding of pepper. Stir and cover. Cook for 4–5 minutes, then remove the scallops from the pan and place them gently in their shells, sprinkling them with the sauce remaining in the frying pan. Season with oil, a pinch of salt and pepper, a slice of lemon (optional) and the remaining parsley.

Divide the scallops, octopuses, mantis shrimps and prawns between four large plates and serve just warm. If you like, you can serve the seafood with a dish of finely minced fresh yellow and red peppers and white onions, seasoned with extra virgin olive oil, balsamic vinegar and salt.

Where no written menu exists, take *'Antipasto di mare'*

Death at La Fenice, pp. 269–274

Padovani was waiting inside the restaurant when Brunetti got there. The journalist stood between the bar and the glass case filled with various antipasti: periwinkles,* cuttlefish,* shrimp.* They shook hands briefly and were shown to their table by Signora Antonia, the Junoesque waitress who reigned supreme here. Once seated, they delayed the discussion of crime and gossip while they consulted with Signora Antonia about lunch. Though a written menu did exist, few regular clients ever bothered with it; most had never seen it. The day's selections and specialities were listed in Antonia's head. She quickly ran through the list, though Brunetti knew that this was the merest of formalities. She quickly decided that what they wanted to eat was the antipasto di mare, the risotto with shrimp,* and the grilled branzino,* which she assured them had come fresh that morning from the fish market. Padovani asked if he might possibly, if the signora advised it, have a green salad as well. She gave his request the attention it deserved, assented, and said they wanted a bottle of the house white wine, which she went to get. (...)

Antonia approached the table with a long metal tray upon which lay their branzino. She placed it on a small serving table next to them and very efficiently cut two portions of tender white fish from it. She placed the portions in front of them. 'I hope you like this.' The men exchanged a glance in silent acceptance of the threat.

'Thank you, Signora,' Padovani said. 'Might I trouble you for the green salad?'

'When you finish the fish,' she said, and went back towards the kitchen.

SHRIMP, MELON AND ROCKET
Gamberetti, melone e rucola

Serves 4
600g (1lb 5oz) shrimps
1 medium melon, weighing about 800g (1¾lb)
a pinch of salt and freshly ground black
6 tablespoons extra virgin olive oil
juice of 1 lemon
60g (2½oz) shelled walnuts
60g (2½oz) rocket

Plunge the washed shrimps into a pan of boiling salted water. After 2 minutes, drain and shell them, then place them in a serving dish. Peel the melon and remove the seeds, then cut into small pieces. Add the melon to the shrimps together with the salt, oil, pepper, lemon juice, walnut kernels, and lastly the rocket leaves. Mix well and serve at room temperature. This is an excellent summer appetizer.

CUTTLEFISH EGGS
Latticini di seppia

Serves 4

1 celery stalk
½ an onion
1 small carrot
coarse salt and freshly ground black pepper
1 bay leaf
500g (1lb 2oz) cuttlefish eggs, cleaned
extra virgin olive oil
a pinch of finely chopped fresh parsley

Put the vegetables into a large pan of water with a bit of coarse salt and the bay leaf, bring to the boil, then reduce the heat a bit and simmer for 45 minutes. Add the cuttlefish eggs and cook for 5 minutes, then drain, discarding the vegetables. When cool, cut the cuttlefish eggs into pieces, removing the elastic film. Place in a bowl and season with a drizzle of olive oil, a bit of salt if needed, a grind of pepper and the parsley. Mix carefully and serve.

A Venetian speciality: Cuttlefish eggs

A Sea of Troubles, pp. 35–38

The plastic strips parted and a young man in black jacket and trousers backed into the room. When he turned around, Brunetti saw that he had a plate of what appeared to be *antipasto di pesce* in each hand. The waiter nodded to the two newcomers and went to the table in the far corner, where he set the two plates down in front of a man and woman in their sixties.

The waiter came back towards their table. Brunetti and Vianello had realized that this was not the sort of place to bother with a menu, at least not this early in the season, so Brunetti smiled and said, as one always does in a new restaurant, 'Everyone says you can eat very well here.' He was careful to speak in Veneziano.

'I hope so,' the waiter said, smiling as he spoke and making no sign that he found the presence of a uniformed policeman in any way surprising.

'What can you recommend today?' Brunetti asked.

'The *antipasto di mare** is good. We've got cuttlefish eggs* or sardines* if you'd like them, instead.'

'What else?' Vianello asked.

'There was still some asparagus in the market this morning, so there's a salad of asparagus and shrimp.'

Brunetti nodded at this; Vianello said he wouldn't have antipasto, so the waiter passed on to the *primi piatti*.

'*Spaghetti alle vongole,** *spaghetti alle cozze,** and *spaghetti all' Amatriciana,**' he recited and then stopped.

'That's all?' Vianello couldn't help asking.

The waiter waved one hand in the air. 'We've got fifty people coming for a wedding anniversary tonight, so we've only got a few things on the menu today.'

Brunetti ordered the *vongole* and Vianello the *all' Amatriciana*.

The choice of main courses was limited to roast turkey or mixed fried fish. Vianello chose the first, Brunetti the second. They ordered a half-litre of white wine and a litre of mineral water. The waiter brought them a basket of *bussolai*, the thick oval breadsticks that Brunetti especially liked.

When he was gone, Brunetti picked one up, broke it in half, and took a bite. It always surprised him how they remained so crisp in this seaside climate. The waiter brought the wine and water, set them on the table, and hurried over to remove the plates from in front of the elderly couple.

'We come out to Pellestrina and you don't eat fish,' Brunetti said, making it a statement rather than a question, though it was.

Vianello poured them each a glass of wine, picked up his, and sipped at it. 'Very good,' he said. 'It's like what my uncle used to bring back from Istria on his boat.'

'And the fish?' Brunetti asked, not letting it go.

'I don't eat it any more,' Vianello said. 'Not unless I know it comes from the Atlantic.' (...)

Neither of them spoke for a long time, and then the waiter was back, bringing Brunetti his antipasto, a small mound of tiny pink shrimp on a bed of slivered raw asparagus. Brunetti took a forkful: they'd been sprinkled with balsamic vinegar. The combination of sweet, sour, sweet, salty was wonderful. Ignoring Vianello for a moment, he ate the salad slowly, relishing it, perpetually delighted by the contrast of flavours and textures.

He set his fork on the plate and took a sip of wine. 'Are you afraid to ruin my meal by telling me what polluting horrors lie in wait for me inside the shrimp?' he asked, smiling.

'Clams are worse,' said Vianello, smiling back but with no further attempt at clarification.

Before Brunetti could ask for a list of the deadly poisons that lurked in his shrimp and clams, the waiter took his plate away, then was quickly back with the two dishes of pasta.

The rest of the meal passed amiably as they talked idly of people they'd known who had fished in the waters around Pellestrina and of a famous footballer from Chioggia whom neither of them had ever seen play. When their main courses came, Vianello could not help giving Brunetti's a suspicious glance, though he had forgone the opportunity to comment further upon the clams. Brunetti, for his part, gave silent proof of the high regard in which he held his sergeant by not repeating to him the contents of an article he had read the previous month about the methods used in commercial turkey farming, nor did he list the transmissible diseases to which those birds are prone.

Marinated Sardines
Sardine in saor

Serves 4

500g (1lb 2oz) sardines
50g (2oz) flour
500g (1lb 2oz) white onions, finely sliced
100ml (3½fl oz) extra virgin olive oil
2 teaspoons salt
50ml (2fl oz) white wine vinegar
40g (1½oz) sultanas
20g (¾oz) pine nuts
500ml (18fl oz) sunflower oil

Remove the heads and scales of the sardines, then gut them and wash them thoroughly, patting dry with kitchen paper. Dust with the flour.

Put the onions into a large non-stick pan with the oil, 50ml (2fl oz) of water and the salt. Cook, stirring, over high a heat for 5 minutes. Add the vinegar and cook for another 5 minutes. Crush the sultanas and add to the pan with the pine nuts. After 2 minutes remove the pan from the heat and leave to cool. The onions should be cooked al dente.

Pour the sunflower oil into a large pan that can be used for frying and bring to the boil. Place the floured sardines in the hot oil and fry until golden. Once cooked, remove from the oil and place gently on kitchen paper to cool. In a terrine, place a layer of onions, followed by a layer of sardines and a small pinch of salt. Repeat the layers, finishing with a layer of onions, and set aside to marinate. The sardines will be ready after 24 hours at the earliest, and will keep for 3–4 days – at first in a cool place, then in the refrigerator.

SQUID SALAD
Insalata di calamari

Serves 4

800g (1¾lb) medium squid
500g (1lb 2oz) potatoes, washed but not peeled
50g (2oz) green olives, stoned and sliced
6 tablespoons extra virgin olive oil
1 teaspoon salt
freshly ground black papper
a sprig of fresh parsley, finely chopped

Carefully clean the squid and slice into medium-sized rings. Place in a pan of boiling salted water for 15 minutes or until tender, then drain. Boil the potatoes in a second pan and drain, then skin them and cut them into fairly large pieces. Place the squid, potatoes and olives in a serving dish and season with the oil, salt, pepper and parsley. Mix gently and serve immediately.

FAGOTTINI WITH SHRIMPS
Fagottini agli scampi

Serves 4

230g (8oz) puff pastry (available frozen)
250g (9oz) shrimps
10 green olives, stoned and finely chopped
1 hard-boiled egg, finely chopped
1 teaspoon tomato purée
1 teaspoon strong paprika
1 tablespoon extra virgin olive oil
a pinch of salt
flour for dusting

Shell the shrimps, removing the dark threads along the back. Wash, dry with kitchen paper, and cut into small pieces. Put them into a bowl with the olives and egg. Blend the tomato purée in a bowl with the oil, paprika and salt and add to the shrimps. Mix gently. Roll out the pastry on a lightly floured surface and cut out into 10 squares about the size of the palm of your hand. In the centre of each square place a heap of the shrimp mixture. Draw the edges of the pastry squares together to form pastry bundles, or fagottini. If necessary, use a few drops of water to seal the tops. Line a baking tin with a sheet of baking parchment and arrange the fagottini side by side, piercing them with a toothpick so they will cook perfectly. Place in a hot (220°C/425°F/ Gas 7) oven and bake for about 18 minutes. Remove from the oven and leave to stand for 5 minutes before serving.

Orecchiette con amorini

Unless a person is born within half an hour's drive of the city of Bari, they should not attempt to make orecchiette by hand. These dear little pasta pieces, the size of a one pound coin, are a speciality of the region, and are made from a mixture of white flour and Apulian hard wheat flour to which no egg is added. The process of making them by hand involves mixing the two types of flour with salt and then gradually dribbling in water until the dough is malleable and neither too wet nor too dry.

I once asked my friend Margharita, who is from Bari, to show me how to do it, and we spent an hour in her kitchen. Now, I'm of a mind that Margharita could probably make orrechiette in her sleep or blindfolded; so it was difficult to slow her down and have her explain each step as she made it. I had the feeling, as I watched her, that Margharita found it as easy to make orecchiette as I find it to tie my shoes.

Before we set to work, she tried to explain the process over a coffee and a few of her home-made biscuits. When the coffee cups were in the sink, she poured the two types of flour into a bowl, measuring by eye, then tossed in a bit of salt and stirred everything around with her hand. She poured it out into a small mound on the kitchen table, then dented the top to turn it into a volcano, into which she began to drop spoonfuls of warm water. As the water dripped, Margharita moved the flour around to absorb it easily, then she began to knead it.

After less than ten minutes, she stopped and declared that the dough was ready. When I asked how she could tell, she said it was ready because it felt right. Like you, I lacked the courage to ask the obvious question, so we moved on to the next step, which was to wrap the dough in a piece of plastic and set it aside for fifteen minutes. (This meant we had time to drink another coffee and eat some more of the biscuits.)

When we were done, Margharita opened the package and cut off a handful of dough, rolled it into a small sausage, then sliced the dough into wheels that seemed to me as thin as pieces of cardboard. I asked to try to do it and managed to slice off tiny wheels – some thick and some thin – which Margharita moved without comment to the side of the table.

Returning to her own wheels, she took one and placed it in the palm of her left hand, then, with a rolling motion of the thumb of her right, turned the disc into a tiny orrechiette, thicker at the edges than at the centre and looking as if it longed to be able to soak up pasta sauce in its tiny, perfect centre cup.

Inspired, I picked up one of the limp discs of pasta and placed it in the centre of my left hand, then rolled across it with my right thumb, as though I'd just been arrested and was having my fingerprints taken. There remained in the centre of my palm, adhering stubbornly to my skin, a flattened pat of dough.

I rubbed at it with the fingers of my right hand and finally got it loose. I picked up another disc and repeated the process, successfully producing yet another mashed pat of dough.

By this time, the remaining pieces of the sausage had been transformed into rows of perfect orecchiette, lined up to dry on a clean kitchen towel, and Margharita was busy rolling another sausage.

Seeing my earnest yet dismal attempts, Margharita placed her floured hand on mine and said, 'Barilla makes very nice ones.' And so I pass on this cooking tip to those who are interested in using, if not hand-making, orecchiette: Barilla makes very nice ones.

First Courses · *Primi piatti*

'Pasta and risotti bring good cheer for a start,
While soup will always warm your heart.'

Venetian cooking is very rich in first courses – simpler in the past, but today more elaborate and colourful.

First courses allow us to enjoy time with family and friends – no one can refuse an invitation to eat spaghetti with garlic, oil and chilli in good company. They're also comforting for those who live alone, since a restorative hot dish can be prepared in no time at all.

But imagination definitely provides the greatest stimulus. These dishes can be combined with an infinite number of ingredients: vegetables, herbs, meat, fish, shellfish, cheese, flowers and fruit.

This is food that is easy, nourishing, convenient and within everyone's reach. A single first course dish can be made in larger quantities, or can constitute part of a more sophisticated multi-course meal.

Roberta Pianaro

FIRST COURSES
Primi piatti

Orecchiette with broccoli   52
Orecchiette con amorini

Orecchiette with broccoli and anchovies   53
Orecchiette con amorini e acciughe

Orecchiette with asparagus   54
Orecchiette agli asparagi

Ruote with aubergine and ricotta   55
Ruote con melanzane e ricotta

Mezze maniche with artichokes   56
Mezze maniche ai carciofi

Farfalle with tuna and peppers   57
Farfalle con tonno e peperoni

Fusilli with green olives   58
Fusilli alle olive verdi

Penne rigate with beans and bacon   61
Penne rigate ai fagioli e pancetta

Penne rigate with tomatoes, bacon, onions and chilli   62
Penne rigate con pomodoro, pancetta, cipolla, peperoncino

Tagliatelle with porcini mushrooms   66
Tagliatelle con funghi porcini

Tagliatelle with peppers and tomatoes   69
Tagliatelle con pepperoni e pomodoro

ORECCHIETTE WITH BROCCOLI
Orecchiette con amorini

Serves 4
800g (1¾lb) broccoli
10 tablespoons extra virgin oilive oil
2 large garlic cloves, finely chopped
1 fresh chilli, cut into small pieces
salt and freshly ground black pepper
350g (12oz) orecchiette
30g (1oz) Parmesan cheese, grated
30g (1oz) pecorino romano cheese, grated

Wash the broccoli and peel the stems. Place it in a pan of boiling salted water and cook until al dente, then drain (keeping the water to cook the pasta in) and cut into pieces. Heat the oil in a large non-stick pan or casserole and brown the garlic with the chilli and a pinch of salt. Add the broccoli and mix well, seasoning with salt and pepper. Cook the pasta in boiling salted water, drain, add to the broccoli and cook, stirring, for 2 minutes. Add the Parmesan and pecorino and serve very hot.

ORECCHIETTE WITH BROCCOLI AND ANCHOVIES
Orecchiette con amorini e acciughe

Serves 4

800g (1¾lb) broccoli
350g (12oz) orecchiette
10 tablespoons extra virgin olive oil
2 large garlic cloves, finely chopped
a pinch of dried chilli flakes
salt and freshly ground black pepper
4 anchovy fillets in oil, chopped
30g (1oz) Parmesan cheese, grated
30g (1oz) pecorino romano cheese, grated

Wash the broccoli and peel the stems. Place it in a pan of boiling salted water and cook until al dente, then drain (reserving the water to cook the pasta) and cut into pieces. Heat the oil in a large non-stick pan or casserole and lightly brown the garlic and chilli, adding a pinch of salt. Add the broccoli and the anchovies and check the seasoning. Cook the pasta in boiling salted water, drain, add to the broccoli and mix gently. Stir in the Parmesan and pecorino cheese and serve very hot.

ORECCHIETTE WITH ASPARAGUS
Orecchiette agli asparagi

Serves 4

8 tablespoons extra virgin olive oil

60g (2½oz) finely chopped shallots

2 teaspoons salt

1kg (2¼lb) medium-sized green asparagus, trimmed and cut into 2–3cm (1 inch) pieces

4 hard-boiled eggs, shelled

350g (12oz) orecchiette

freshly ground black pepper

60g (2½oz) Parmesan cheese, grated

In a large non-stick pan or casserole, heat the oil and brown the shallots with the salt and 2 tablespoons of water. Add the asparagus and 800ml (1 pint 8¾fl oz) of lukewarm water. Mix well and cook, covered, over a moderate heat for around 30 minutes. The asparagus should be very tender, with a bit of juice at the bottom. Put the eggs in a bowl, mash with a fork and set aside. Cook the pasta in boiling salted water, drain, and add to the pan with the asparagus. Stir, adding a pinch of pepper and the Parmesan, then pour into a hot serving dish and sprinkle with the mashed eggs.

RUOTE WITH AUBERGINE AND RICOTTA
Ruote con melanzane e ricotta

Serves 4

2–3 aubergines about 15cm (6 inches) long
1 teaspoon salt, plus extra for salting the aubergines
sunflower oil for frying
350g (12oz) ruote or fusilli
8 tablespoons extra virgin olive oil
2 garlic cloves, finely chopped
500g (1lb 2oz) tomatoes, peeled and chopped
1 fresh chilli
10 fresh basil leaves
130g (4½oz) mild ricotta cheese
30g (1oz) pecorino romano cheese, grated

Slice the aubergines into rounds about 1cm (½ inch) thick. Arrange them in layers in a colander and sprinkle each layer with salt. Leave to drain, with a heavy weight on top to press out any excess water. After about 2 hours, squeeze them and pat dry with kitchen paper. Fry, a few at a time, in boiling oil, until golden. Drain on kitchen paper, set aside covered. Cook the pasta in boiling salted water and drain.

For the sauce, heat the olive oil in a large non-stick pan or casserole and lightly brown the garlic. Add the tomatoes, salt, chilli, torn basil leaves and 100ml (3½fl oz) of water. When cooked, blend in the ricotta and add the pasta, aubergines (in whole slices or cut in smaller pieces, as desired) and pecorino. Mix well and serve.

MEZZE MANICHE WITH ARTICHOKES
Mezze maniche ai carciofi

Serves 4
For the pasta
350g (12oz) mezze maniche or penne rigate
60g (2½oz) Parmesan cheese, grated
extra virgin olive oil

For the artichokes
8 medium globe artichokes
½ lemon
6 tablespoons extra virgin olive oil
1 teaspoon salt
1 garlic clove, halved
a handful of fresh parsley, finely chopped
freshly ground black pepper

For this pasta dish, use the recipe for Artichokes Cooked in a Casserole (page 131) but do not boil completely dry; leave a bit of sauce at the bottom of the casserole. Cut the cooked artichokes in thin slices lengthways and return them to the casserole, cutting them up further with a fork. Add a little extra virgin olive oil and return the casserole to the heat. Cook the pasta in boiling salted water and drain. Add to the artichokes, sprinkle with Parmesan and stir. Remove from the heat and serve.

FARFALLE WITH TUNA AND PEPPERS
Farfalle con tonno e peperoni

Serves 4

350g (12oz) farfalle

2 or 3 very fleshy yellow peppers, about 650g (1½lb)

8 tablespoons extra virgin olive oil

1 shallot, finely chopped

2 teaspoons salt

a pinch of dried chilli flakes

450g (1lb) tomatoes, peeled and chopped

150g (5oz) drained tuna, cut into small pieces

Wash and dry the peppers and grill over a burner or under the grill. When charred, leave to cool for a while then scrape off the black skin with a knife. Cut into small pieces and set aside. To make the sauce, heat the oil in a large non-stick pan or casserole and add the shallot, salt, chilli and tomatoes. Cook, adding a bit of hot water from time to time to make a creamy sauce. Stir in the peppers and finally the tuna and keep hot. Cook the pasta in boiling salted water and drain, then add to the sauce and serve.

FUSILLI WITH GREEN OLIVES
Fusilli alle olive verdi

Serves 4
8 tablespoons extra virgin olive oil
2 celery stalks, finely chopped
1 carrot, finely chopped
1 shallot, finely chopped
1–2 teaspoons salt
a pinch of dried chilli flakes
130g (4½oz) green olives, stoned and finely chopped
350g (12oz) fusilli
40g (1½oz) Parmesan cheese, grated

Heat the oil in a large non-stick pan or casserole and add the celery, carrot, shallot, salt and chilli. Cover and cook for 30 minutes over medium heat, adding a little hot water from time to time. When the vegetables are cooked, add the olives and leave to simmer for 2 minutes. The resulting sauce should be fairly thick. Cook the pasta in boiling salted water and drain. Stir into the olive sauce, add the Parmesan and serve.

Eating fusilli on the terrace

The Girl of His Dreams, pp. 54–56

One of the children, no doubt in a moment of suicidal optimism, had decided they should have lunch on the terrace. Without even closing the door, Brunetti took three steps down the corridor and, sticking his head into the living room, called out to the three of them, now seated outdoors and waiting for him: 'My chair goes in the sun.' By this time of year, the sun appeared on their large terrace for a few hours each day, the period growing longer as the year advanced. But in these first weeks it fell only on the far end of the terrace and then for just two hours, one on either side of true noon. So only one chair could be placed in the sun, and since Brunetti considered it an act of sovereign madness to eat outside this early in the year, he always claimed that seat as his own.

Having staked his claim once again, he went back and shut the front door. From the terrace, he heard scraping sounds. Here in the living room, the sun had been coming in for much of the morning.

His place, the sun shining on to the back of the chair, was at the head of the table. He walked towards it, patting Chiara's shoulder as he passed her. Chiara wore a light sweater, Raffi only a cotton shirt, though Paola wore both a sweater and a down vest he thought belonged to Raffi. How was it that parents as cold-blooded as he and Paola had produced these two tropical creatures?

He was instantly glad of the warmth on his back. Paola reached for Chiara's plate and, from a large bowl in the centre of the table, spooned up fusilli with green olives and mozzarella: it was a bit early in the season for a dish like this, but Brunetti rejoiced in the sight and scent of it. After setting the plate in front of Chiara, she passed her a small dish of whole basil leaves: Chiara took a few and ripped them into small pieces to sprinkle over the top of the pasta.

Paola then served Raffi and Brunetti, both of whom added torn basil leaves to their pasta, and then she served herself. Before she sat down, she set the spoon aside and covered the bowl of pasta with a plate.

'*Buon appetito*,' Paola said and began to eat. Brunetti took a few bites, letting his whole body remember the taste. The last time they had eaten this dish had been towards the end of the summer, when he had opened one of the last bottles of the Masi rosato to go with it. Was it too early in the year for rosato? he wondered. Then he saw the bottle on the table and recognized the colour and the label.

PENNE RIGATE WITH BEANS AND BACON
Penne rigate ai fagioli e pancetta

Serves 4
250g (9oz) tinned pinto beans, drained
5 tablespoons extra virgin olive oil
a pinch of finely chopped fresh rosemary leaves
salt
1 fresh chilli, chopped
200g (7oz) smoked bacon, diced
350g (12oz) penne rigate
60g (2½oz) Parmesan cheese, grated

Put the beans into a bowl with 3 tablespoons of olive oil, the rosemary, a pinch of salt and the chilli. Set aside. In a large non-stick pan or casserole, heat the remaining 2 tablespoons of olive oil and add the diced bacon. When crisp, add the beans and stir. Cook the pasta in boiling salted water and drain. Add it to the pan and cook briskly for 2 minutes. Sprinkle with the Parmesan and serve.

Penne Rigate with Tomatoes, Bacon, Onions and Chilli
Penne rigate con pomodoro, pancetta, cipolla, peperoncino

Serves 4

10 tablespoons extra virgin olive oil
100g (3½oz) onion, thinly sliced
2 sprigs of fresh rosemary
salt
2 fresh chillies, cut into small pieces
600g (1lb 5oz) ripe tomatoes, chopped
100ml (3½fl oz) dry white wine
350g (12oz) penne rigate
150g (5oz) mild bacon, diced
1 bay leaf
50g (2½oz) Parmesan cheese, grated

Heat the oil in a large non-stick pan or casserole and add the onion, 1 sprig of rosemary, a pinch of salt, the chillies, and a little water. Cook gently until the onion becomes transparent, gradually adding the tomatoes and wine to make a thick, smooth sauce. Adjust the seasoning with salt. Cook the pasta in boiling salted water and drain. Meanwhile put the diced bacon, the second sprig of rosemary and the bay leaf into a small pan and cook over a low heat until the bacon is crisp. Drain the pasta and toss gently with the sauce and bacon, then sprinkle with the Parmesan and serve very hot.

Brunetti's favourite pasta: *Penne rigate*

The Anonymous Venetian, pp. 148–151

'*A tavola, tutti a tavola. Mangiamo*,' Padovani called. Brunetti closed the book, set it aside, and went over to take his place at the table. 'You sit there, on the left,' Padovani said. He set the bowl down and started immediately to heap pasta on to the plate in front of Brunetti.

Brunetti looked down, waited until Padovani had served himself, and began to eat. Tomato, onion, cubes of *pancetta*, and perhaps a touch of *peperoncino*, all poured over *penne rigate*, his favourite dried pasta.

'It's good,' he said, meaning it. 'I like the *peperoncino*.'

'Oh, good. I never know if people are going to think it's too hot.'

'No, it's perfect,' Brunetti said and continued to eat. When he had finished his helping and Padovani was putting more on to his plate, Brunetti said, 'His name's Francesco Crespo.'

'I should have known,' said Padovani with a tired sigh. Then, sounding far more interested, he asked, 'You sure there's not too much *peperoncino*?'

Brunetti shook his head and finished his second portion, then held out his hands to cover his plate when Padovani reached for the serving spoon.

'You better. There's hardly anything else,' Padovani insisted.

'No, really, Damiano.'

'Suit yourself, but Paola's not to blame me if you starve to death while she's away.' He picked up their two plates, set them inside the serving bowl, and went back into the kitchen.

He was to emerge twice before he sat down again. The first time, he carried a small roast of ground turkey breast wrapped in *pancetta* and surrounded by potatoes, and the second a plate of mixed salad greens.

'That's all there is,' he said when he sat down, and Brunetti suspected that he was meant to read it as an apology.

Brunetti helped himself to the roast meat and potatoes and began to eat.

Padovani filled their glasses and helped himself to both turkey and potatoes. 'Crespo came originally from, I think, Mantova. He moved to Padova about four years ago, to study pharmacy. But he quickly learned that life was far more interesting if he followed his natural inclination and set himself up as a whore, and he soon discovered that the best way to do that was to find himself an older man who would support him. The usual stuff: an apartment, a car, plenty of money for clothes, and in return all he had to do was be there when the man who paid the bills was able to get away from the bank, or the city council meeting, or his wife. I think he was only about eighteen at the time. And very, very pretty.' Padovani paused with his fork in the air. 'In fact, he reminded me then of the Bacchus of Caravaggio: beautiful, but too knowing and just on the edge of corruption.'

Padovani offered some peppers to Brunetti and took some himself. 'The last thing I know about him at first hand was that he was mixed up with an accountant from Treviso. But Franco could never keep himself from straying, and the accountant threw him out. Beat him up, I think, and threw him out. I don't know when he started with the transvestism; that sort of thing has never interested me in the least. In fact, I suppose I don't understand it. If you want a woman, then have a woman.'

'Maybe it's a way to deceive yourself that it is a woman,' Brunetti suggested, using Paola's theory and thinking, now, that it made sense.

'Perhaps. But how sad, eh?' Padovani moved his plate to the side and sat back. 'I mean, we deceive ourselves all the time, about whether we love someone, or why we do, or why we tell the lies we do. But you'd think we could at least be honest with ourselves about who we want to go to bed with. It seems little enough, that.' He picked up the salad and sprinkled salt on it, poured olive oil liberally over the leaves, then added a splash of vinegar.

Brunetti handed him his plate and accepted the clean salad plate he was given in its place. Padovani pushed the bowl towards him. 'Help yourself. There's no dessert. Only fruit.'

'I'm glad you didn't have to go to any trouble,' Brunetti said, and Padovani laughed.

'Well, I really did have all of this in the house. Except for the fruit.'

Brunetti took a very small portion of salad; Padovani took even less.

'What else do you know about Crespo?' Brunetti asked.

Tagliatelle with Porcini Mushrooms
Tagliatelle con funghi porcini

Serves 4

300g (11oz) tagliatelle or pappardelle
600g (1lb 5oz) porcini mushrooms
8 tablespoons extra virgin olive oil
1 garlic clove, finely chopped
½ teaspoon salt
a pinch of finely chopped parsley
15g (½oz) butter
50ml (2fl oz) fresh cream
50g (2oz) Parmesan cheese, grated
freshly ground black pepper

Wash the mushrooms and cut into medium-sized pieces. In a non-stick casserole, heat the oil and add the garlic and salt. Cook for a few minutes, being careful not to burn the garlic. Add the mushrooms, stir and continue cooking over a high heat. Add the parsley and stir frequently. The mushrooms will be ready when their own water has evaporated and there is only oil left at the bottom of the casserole. Add the butter, cream, pepper, and more salt if necessary, and cook until the sauce thickens slightly. Cook the pasta in boiling salted water and drain. Add to the sauce with the Parmesan. Stir gently and serve very hot.

Tagliatelle with porcini: a taste you can fully appreciate only when in a good mood

Fatal Remedies, pp. 86–87

He walked up the embankment towards the Greek church, crossed the bridge, and went into the bar that stood facing him.

'*Buon giorno*, Commissario,' the barman greeted him. '*Cosa desidera?*'

Before knowing what to order, Brunetti looked down at his watch. He'd lost all sense of time and was surprised to see that it was almost noon. '*Un'ombra*,' he answered and, when it came, drank the small glass of white wine without bothering to sip or taste it. It didn't help at all, and he had sense enough to know that another would help even less. He dropped a thousand lire on the counter and went back to the Questura.

He spoke to no one, merely went up to his office and got his coat, then left again and went home.

At lunch, it was clear that Paola had told the children about what had happened. Chiara looked at her mother with obvious confusion, but it seemed that Raffi looked at her with interest, perhaps even curiosity. No one brought up the subject, so the meal passed in relative calm. Ordinarily, Brunetti would have rejoiced in the fresh tagliatelle and porcini, but today he barely tasted them. Nor did he much enjoy the spezzatini and fried melanzane* which followed. When they had finished, Chiara went to her piano lesson and Raffi to his friend's to study maths.

Alone, the table still littered with plates and serving bowls, Paola and Brunetti drank their coffee, his laced with grappa, hers black and sweet. 'You going to get a lawyer?' he asked.

TAGLIATELLE WITH PEPPERS AND TOMATOES
Tagliatelle con peperoni e pomodoro

Serves 4
250g (9oz) dried tagliatelle
10 tablespoons extra virgin olive oil
3–4 yellow peppers, deseeded and cut in strips
100g (3½oz) white onions, thinly sliced
400g (14oz) tomatoes, peeled and chopped
salt and freshly ground black pepper
30g (1oz) Parmesan cheese, grated

Heat the oil in a large non-stick pan or casserole and add the peppers, onion and tomatoes along with a pinch of salt. Cook over a moderate heat, stirring frequently, for at least 20–25 minutes. Cook the pasta in boiling salted water and drain. Add to the pan and stir in the Parmesan and a good grind of pepper. Serve at once.

Spaghetti All'amatriciana
Spaghetti all'amatriciana

Serves 4
6 tablespoons extra virgin olive oil
½ a white onion, finely chopped
a pinch of salt
1 fresh chilli, chopped
5 tomatoes, peeled and chopped
200g (7oz) smoked bacon, diced
350g (12oz) spaghetti or penne
60g (2½oz) pecorino romano cheese, grated

Heat 5 tablespoons of the oil in a large non-stick pan or casserole and fry the onion with the salt, chilli, and 2 tablespoons of water. When the onion is transparent, add the tomatoes and continue to cook, adding a little water from time to time to make a creamy sauce. Heat the remaining tablespoon of oil in a small pan and fry the bacon until crisp. Cook the pasta in boiling salted water and drain. Add to the sauce along with the bacon and its sauce. Stir in the pecorino and serve very hot.

SPAGHETTI WITH OLIVES AND MOZZARELLA
Spaghetti con olive e mozzarella

Serves 4

350g (12oz) spaghetti
8 tablespoons extra virgin olive oil
2 garlic cloves, finely chopped
1 fresh chilli, or 2 if preferred, chopped
salt
700g (1½lb) ripe tomatoes, peeled and chopped
70g (2¾oz) dried black olives, stoned and chopped
60g (2½oz) Parmesan cheese, grated
250g (9oz) mozzarella cheese, diced
10 fresh basil leaves, torn into strips

Heat the oil in a large non-stick pan or casserole and add the garlic, chilli, a pinch of salt and the tomatoes. Stir and cook over a high heat to make a creamy sauce. Add the olives and half the basil; adjust the seasoning with salt. Cook the pasta in boiling salted water and drain, then add to the casserole and stir over a low heat until combined. Sprinkle with the Parmesan and stir well. Add the remaining basil and the mozzarella and serve very hot.

SPAGHETTI WITH MUSSELS
Spaghetti alle cozze

Serves 4
350g (12oz) spaghetti
1.5kg (3¼lb) mussels
6 tablespoons extra virgin olive oil
1 garlic clove, finely chopped
salt and freshly ground black pepper
800g (1¾lb) tomatoes, chopped
a pinch of finely chopped parsley

Wash the mussels, remove their beards, drain them and place in a large non-stick pan. Cook, covered, over a high heat until they open. Remove the mussels from their shells and discard the shells. Cut the largest mussels into pieces. Strain the liquid remaining in the pan and pour into a bowl. In the same (washed) non-stick pan, heat the oil and add the garlic, a pinch of salt and the tomatoes. Simmer the sauce for 20 minutes, until reduced and add the mussel liquid. Add the mussels and finally the parsley. Mix and season. Cook the pasta in boiling salted water and drain. Add to the hot sauce along with a good grind of pepper, stir and serve.

Spaghetti with Clams
Spaghetti alle vongole

Serves 4
350g (12oz) spaghetti
1.5kg (3¼lb) clams
8 tablespoons extra virgin olive oil
2 garlic cloves, halved
salt
1 fresh chilli, chopped
a pinch of finely chopped parsley

Wash the clams, put them into a large bowl of water and leave to soak for 2 hours. Drain them, then place in a large lidded pan or casserole and cook over a high heat until they all open. Strain their liquid into a bowl. Once cooled, remove the clams from their shells and place them in the bowl with their liquid. Heat the oil in another non-stick pan or casserole and add the garlic, salt and chilli, browning without burning. Discard the garlic and remove the casserole from the heat to avoid hot oil splashes. Add the clams and their liquid, together with the parsley. Cook, stirring, for 2 minutes. Cook the pasta in boiling salted water and drain. Add it to the clams, heat, stirring gently, and serve. If desired, this dish can be garnished with a few clam shells.

Bigoli in Sauce
Bigoli in salsa

Serves 4
10 very fleshy anchovies, preserved in salt
50ml (2fl oz) extra virgin olive oil
400g (14oz) white onions, thinly sliced
a small pinch of salt
350g (12oz) spaghetti

Wash the anchovies thoroughly. Cut them in half and remove the bones, then place them between 2 or more sheets of kitchen paper and leave to dry. Heat the oil in a large non-stick pan and add the onions, a pinch of salt and 100ml (3½fl oz) of water. Cook over medium heat, stirring often and adding 200ml (7fl oz) of water, a little at a time. When the onions are almost wilted (and this is the secret of the sauce), add the anchovies and blend in. Adjust the seasoning with salt if necessary. Cook the pasta in boiling salted water and drain. Add to the hot sauce, mix gently and serve at once.

Basic Recipe for Pancakes
Ricetta base per le crespelle

Serves 6 (12 pancakes)
200g (7oz) flour
2 eggs
½ teaspoon salt
300ml (½ pint) milk
30g (1oz) butter, melted

Place the flour, eggs and salt in a bowl and mix. Add the milk, a little at a time, and finally the melted butter. The resulting blend should be a fairly liquid, lump-free cream. (If not, use a whisk to remedy.) Leave to rest, covered, for 1 hour.

Place a non-stick frying pan 22cm (9 inches) in diameter over a high heat and add 100ml (3½fl oz) of the batter, spreading it over the entire surface. After a few seconds the pancake will start to set. Turn it with a spatula and continue cooking on the other side, very briefly. It only takes a few seconds to cook. Continue in the same way with the rest of the batter. Arrange the pancakes, one on top of the other, on a plate. When cold, wrap them in clingfilm to stop them drying out.

PANCAKES WITH SPINACH AND RICOTTA
Crespelle agli spinaci e ricotta

Serves 6

12 pancakes (see page 75)
750g (1lb 10oz) frozen spinach
4 tablespoons extra virgin olive oil
60g (2½oz) shallots, finely chopped
1 teaspoon salt
250g (9oz) mild ricotta cheese
250ml (8fl oz) fresh cream
70g (2¾oz) Parmesan cheese, grated

Make the pancakes according to the basic recipe on p. 75.

Thaw the spinach and squeeze well to get rid of excess water. Heat the oil in a non-stick pan and fry the shallots with the salt and a bit of water. Add the spinach and cook until any excess liquid has evaporated. Leave to cool, then stir in the ricotta. Divide the mixture into 12 portions, spread one on to each pancake and roll them up. Place them side by side in an ovenproof dish, add the cream and sprinkle with the Parmesan. Put into a hot oven (240°C/475°F/Gas 9) and bake for about 20 minutes. The pancake rolls should be golden in colour. Serve hot.

Pancakes with Green Asparagus
Crespelle agli asparagi verdi

Serves 6

12 pancakes (see page 75)
4 tablespoons extra virgin olive oil
100g (3½oz) white onion, finely chopped
1 teaspoon salt
800g (1¾lb) green asparagus, tender parts only, cut in pieces
250g (9oz) mild ricotta cheese
250ml (8fl oz) fresh cream
70g (2¾oz) Parmesan cheese, grated

Make the pancakes according to the basic recipe on p. 75.

Heat the oil in a non-stick pan and add the onion, the salt and 600ml (1 pint) of water. Add the asparagus and cook, covered, over a moderate heat until fork-tender, stirring from time to time. Remove the lid, reduce the mixture, leave to cool then stir in the ricotta. Divide the mixture into 12 portions, spread one on to each pancake and roll them up. Arrange them side by side in an ovenproof dish, add the cream and sprinkle with the Parmesan. Place in a hot oven (240ºC/475ºF/Gas 9) and bake for about 20 minutes. The pancake rolls should be golden in colour. Serve hot.

Lasagne with Artichoke Hearts and Prosciutto
Lasagne con cuori di carciofo e prosciutto

Serves 6
8 medium globe artichokes
1 garlic clove, halved
8 tablespoons extra virgin olive oil
½ a lemon, squeezed
1 teaspoon salt
a pinch of finely chopped fresh parsley
12 dry lasagne sheets
200g (7oz) prosciutto, cooked and finely chopped
100g (3½oz) Parmesan cheese, grated
butter for the baking tin

For the béchamel sauce
75g (2¾oz) butter
75g (2¾oz) flour
750ml (1¼ pints) hot milk
a pinch of salt
a grind of nutmeg

Cut off the artichoke stems and peel. Remove all the tough leaves from the artichokes and trim the tips thoroughly. As you work, place the artichokes in a bowl of cold water with the lemon juice (to prevent discoloration). Drain and arrange the artichokes side by side in a non-stick casserole with the stems, oil, garlic, salt and 750ml (1¼ pint) of water. Cover and place over a high heat. When the water comes to the boil, add the parsley, reduce the heat to medium and cook for 30 minutes. Remove the lid and boil off the remaining water so that only the oil is left at the bottom. Set aside to cool.

To make the béchamel sauce, use a non-stick pan with high sides. Melt the butter over a moderate heat and stir in the flour. Remove the pan from the heat and gradually add the hot milk, stirring all the time. Return the pan to the heat and cook gently, stirring, until the sauce thickens. Adjust the seasoning with salt, add a grind of nutmeg and set aside to cool. (If lumps should form, dissolve them with a whisk or egg beater.)

Plunge the lasagne sheets into a pan of boiling salted water and leave for 1 minute. Remove from the heat and place under cold running water, removing the lasagne sheets with a slotted spoon and placing them on a large plate.

Place the artichokes on a chopping board and remove the large leaves. Finely chop the hearts and stems and place in a bowl with the prosciutto.

Now prepare the lasagne: butter a 26 x 19cm (10 x 7.5 inch) baking tin and arrange 3 lasagne sheets on the base. Cover them with a layer of béchamel sauce, then a layer of the artichoke/prosciutto mix and a sprinkle of Parmesan. Repeat, starting each layer with 3 lasagne sheets; finish with just béchamel and Parmesan on top of the last layer. Place in a hot oven and bake for about 20 minutes at a high temperature. The surface of the lasagne should be golden and bubbling. Cool slightly before serving.

Lasagne, the recipe of Brunetti's mother

Through a Glass, Darkly, pp. 160–163

On the kitchen table, he found a note from Paola, saying she had to meet one of the students whose doctoral work she was overseeing but that there was lasagne in the oven. The kids would not be home, and a salad was in the refrigerator: all he had to do was add oil and vinegar. Just as Brunetti was preparing to start grumbling his way through lunch – having come halfway across the city, only to be deprived of the company of his family, forced to eat heated-up things from the oven, probably made with some sort of pre-packaged whatever and that disgusting orange American cheese for all he knew – he saw the last line of Paola's note: 'Stop sulking. It's your mother's recipe and you love it.'

Left to eat alone, Brunetti's first concern was to find the right thing to read. A magazine would be right, but he had already finished that week's *Espresso*. A newspaper took up too much space on the table. A paperback book could never be forced to stay open, not without breaking the binding completely, which would later cause the pages to fall out. Art books, which were surely big enough, suffered from oil stains. He compromised by going into the bedroom and taking from his bedside Gibbon, whose style forced him to read in translation.

He took out the lasagne, cut it and put a chunk on a plate. He poured a glass of Pinot grigio then opened Gibbon to his place and propped it up against two books Paola had left on the table. He employed a cutting board and a serving spoon to hold the pages open on both sides. Satisfied with the arrangement, he sat down and started to eat.

Brunetti found himself back in the court of the Emperor

Heliogabalus, one of his favourite monsters. Ah, the excess of it, the violence, the utter corruption of everything and everyone. The lasagne had layers of ham and thin slices of artichoke hearts interleaved with layers of pasta that he suspected might have been home made. He would have preferred more artichokes. He shared his table with decapitated senators, evil counsellors, barbarians bent on the destruction of the empire. He took a sip of wine and ate another bite of lasagne.

The Emperor appeared, arrayed like the sun itself. All hailed him, his glory, and his graciousness. The court was splendid and excessive, a place where, as Gibbon observed, 'a capricious prodigality supplied the want of taste and elegance'. Brunetti set his fork down, the better to savour both the lasagne and Gibbon's description.

He got up and took the salad, poured oil and vinegar and sprinkled in some salt. He ate from the bowl, as Heliogabalus died under the swords of his guards.

Lasagne with Meat Sauce and Peas

Lasagne al ragù e piselli

Serves 6

For the peas

5 tablespoons extra virgin olive oil
50g (2oz) onion, finely chopped
½ teaspoon salt
350g (12oz) frozen peas

For the meat sauce

50g (2oz) onion, finely chopped
50g (2oz) celery, finely chopped
50g (2oz) carrot, finely chopped
8 tablespoons extra virgin olive oil
1 teaspoon salt
250g (9oz) lean pork, minced
50ml (2fl oz) dry white wine
400g (14oz) tinned tomatoes
100g (3½oz) cooked prosciutto, finely chopped
a pinch of freshly ground black pepper

For the béchamel sauce

50g (2oz) butter
50g (2oz) flour
½ teaspoon salt
500ml (18fl oz) hot milk
a pinch of ground nutmeg

For the pasta
12 sheets of dry lasagne
100g (3½oz) Parmesan, grated
butter for the baking tin

Place the oil, onion, salt and 2 tablespoons of water in a non-stick pan and cook for 2–3 minutes. Add the peas and cook over a high heat, stirring frequently, for another 15 minutes.

To make the meat sauce, place all the chopped vegetables in a non-stick casserole with the oil, salt, and 2 tablespoons of water, cooking for 5 minutes. Add the pork, mix, and cook for a bit longer. Add the wine, let the alcohol evaporate and add the tomatoes. Cover and cook over low heat for at least 1½ hours, adding hot water from time to time. Then add the prosciutto, increase the heat, add the pepper and reduce the sauce; only the oil should appear at the bottom of the casserole now. Add the peas, mix, and set aside.

To make the béchamel, melt the butter in a narrow pan with high sides. Add the flour and salt, blending to a paste. Remove the pan from the heat and add the hot milk, a little at a time. Return the pan to moderate heat and thicken the béchamel, stirring constantly and adding the nutmeg at the end. (If lumps should form, dissolve them with a whisk or egg beater.)

Plunge the lasagne sheets into a pan of boiling salted water and leave for 1 minute. Remove from the heat and place under cold running water, removing the lasagne sheets with a slotted spoon and placing them, side by side, on a dry tea towel. Butter a 26 x 13cm (10 x 5 inch) baking tin and arrange the first layer of the lasagne: 3 lasagne sheets, a layer of meat sauce, then a sprinkle of Parmesan. Repeat, starting each layer with 3 lasagne sheets. Cover the last layer of lasagne with the béchamel and a final dusting of cheese. Place in a hot oven (240°C/475°F/Gas 9) and bake for about 20 minutes. The surface should be golden. Cool slightly before serving for even more flavour.

Ravioli with Mushrooms
Ravioli con funghi

Serves 4

2 tablespoons extra virgin olive oil
½ a garlic clove, finely chopped
salt
300g (11oz) mixed mushrooms
70g (2¾oz) Parmesan cheese, grated
200g (7oz) flour, plus a handful for the pastry board
a little semolina
2 medium eggs
1 egg white
40g (1½oz) butter
200g (7oz) robiola cheese

Heat the oil in a non-stick pan and fry the garlic with a pinch of salt. Add the mushrooms and cook until they are completely dry, leaving only the oil at the bottom of the pan. Remove from the heat and cool. Once cooled, place the mixture in a bowl and reduce to a purée with a blender. Add 3 tablespoons of Parmesan.

Put the flour in another bowl, placing the eggs in the centre, and knead. Once the dough is smooth and elastic, place it on the floured pastry board, knead again, and roll out into a thin sheet with a rolling pin. Cut into about 50 circles measuring 7cm (3 inches) in diameter. Arrange them side by side on a flat surface floured with semolina. While they are still soft, proceed with the stuffing. Place hazelnut-size mounds of the mushroom filling in the middle of each round of dough. Dampen the circumference of the rounds with the egg white, fold them in two and seal, pressing together carefully with your fingers so they will not open during cooking. Cook the ravioli in plenty of boiling salted water for 2–3 minutes and drain. Arrange them on hot plates, sprinkle with the remaining Parmesan, and top with the butter and robiola cheese, both just melted.

What Chiara tried to cook: *Ravioli con funghi*

A Noble Radiance, pp. 110–117

He hung his coat in the cupboard in the hall and went down the long corridor towards the kitchen. Chiara turned towards him as he came in.

'*Ciao, Papà. Mamma*'s teaching me how to make ravioli. We're going to have them tonight.' She held her flour-covered hands behind her back and came a few steps towards him. He leaned down and she kissed him on both cheeks; he wiped a long smear of flour from her left cheek. 'Filled with *funghi*, right *Mamma*?' she asked, turning to Paola, who stood at the stove, stirring the mushrooms in a large frying pan. She nodded and kept stirring.

Behind them on the table lay a few crooked piles of oddly shaped pale rectangles. 'Are those the ravioli?' he asked, remembering the neat geometry of the squares his mother used to cut and fill.

'They will be, *Papà*, as soon as we get them filled.' She turned to Paola for confirmation. 'Won't they, *Mamma*?'

Paola stirred and nodded, turned to Brunetti and accepted his kisses without comment.

'Won't they, *Mamma*?' Chiara repeated, voice a tone higher.

'Yes. Just a few more minutes for the mushrooms and we can start to fill them.'

'You said I could do it myself, *Mamma*,' Chiara insisted.

Before Chiara could turn to Brunetti to witness this injustice, Paola conceded the point. 'If your father will pour me a glass of wine while the mushrooms finish, all right?' (. . .)

Chiara was in the kitchen, muttering dark threats at the pieces of ravioli which refused to maintain the shape into which she squeezed them. He said goodbye and went down the hall to Paola's study. He stuck his head inside and said, 'If it's necessary, we can always go over to Gianni's for pizza.'

She glanced up from her papers. 'No matter what she does to those poor ravioli, we are going to eat every one she puts on our plates, and you are going to ask for seconds.' Before he could protest, she cut him off, pointing a threatening pencil at him. 'It's the first dinner she's cooked, all by herself, and it's going to be wonderful.' She saw him start to speak and cut him off again. 'Burned mushrooms, pasta that will have the consistency of wallpaper glue, and a chicken that she's chosen to marinate in soy sauce and which will consequently have the salt content of the Dead Sea.'

'You make it sound inviting.' Well, Brunetti thought, she can't do anything with the wine. 'What about Raffi? How are you going to get him to eat it?'

'Don't you think he loves his little sister?' she asked with the false indignation he knew so well.

Brunetti said nothing.

'All right,' Paola admitted, 'I promised him ten thousand lire if he ate everything.'

'Me too?' Brunetti asked and left.

Ravioli with Squash, Butter and Sage
Ravioli di zucca con burro e salvia

Serves 4

For the stuffing

250g (9oz) squash, peeled and cut into pieces
a pinch of salt
30g (1oz) shallots, finely chopped
4 tablespoons extra virgin olive oil
40g (1½oz) Parmesan cheese, grated
3 macaroons, crushed

For the pastry

200g (7oz) flour, plus a handful for the pastry board
2 eggs, each around 65g (2½oz)
1 egg white to seal the ravioli

For the seasoning

150g (5oz) butter
8 sage leaves
40g (1½oz) Parmesan cheese, grated

Place the squash in a non-stick pan or casserole with the salt, shallot, oil and 400ml (14fl oz) of water. Cook, covered, over a moderate heat at first, then increase the heat and stir to obtain a fairly thick purée. When the mixture has cooled, sprinkle with the Parmesan and add the crushed macaroons. Stir gently and set aside.

Put the flour in a bowl, break the eggs into the centre, and knead. Once the dough is smooth and elastic, set it aside, covered, for 1 hour. Place the dough on a floured pastry board, knead again, and roll out into a thin sheet with a wooden rolling pin. Cut into 40 circles or more, 7cm (3 inches) in diameter. (This can be done using a thin-edged glass.) Arrange them side by side on a lightly floured flat surface. While they are still soft, proceed with the stuffing. Place half a teaspoon of the squash purée in the middle of each round of dough. Dampen the edges of the rounds with the egg white, fold them in two and seal, pressing together carefully with your fingers so they will not open during cooking.

Place the butter and sage in a small non-stick pan, melting the butter without burning it. Serve the ravioli on hot plates and pour over the sage butter. Sprinkle with the Parmesan and serve immediately.

Risotto with Squash Blossoms and Ginger
Risotto di fiori di zucca e zenzero

Serves 4
350g (12oz) squash blossoms
3 tablespoons extra virgin olive oil
2 shallots, finely chopped
1 teaspoon salt
2 teaspoons crushed meat stock cube
30g (1oz) fresh ginger root, peeled and grated
320g (11½oz) risotto rice, e.g. Carnaroli, Arborio, Vialone Nano
30g (1oz) butter
30g (1oz) Parmesan cheese, grated

Wash the squash blossoms. Keep the pistils and cut the petals. Heat the oil in a non-stick casserole and fry the shallots lightly together with the salt and 2 tablespoons of water. When transparent, add the squash blossoms and pistils and 200ml (7fl oz) water and cook for 15 minutes. Add the crushed stock cube and 1 teaspoon of the ginger. Add the rice and cook, adding 1 litre (1¾ pints) of boiling water, 200ml (7fl oz) at a time. Cook for 20–30 minutes until al dente, then add the remaining ginger and mix well. Add the butter and Parmesan, and serve.

Risotto with Squash
Risotto di zucca

Serves 4

6 tablespoons extra virgin olive oil
1 shallot, finely chopped
1 teaspoon salt
400g (14oz) squash, peeled and cut into pieces
2 teaspoons crushed meat stock cube
320g (11½oz) risotto rice, e.g. Carnaroli, Arborio, Vialone Nano
20g (¾oz) butter
30g (1oz) Parmesan cheese, grated

Heat the oil in a large non-stick pan or casserole and fry the shallot lightly with the salt and 2 tablespoons of water. When transparent, add the squash, 800ml (1 pint 8¾fl oz) of water and the crushed stock cube. Cover and cook for 30 minutes. When the squash is very creamy, add the rice. Cook, stirring continually and adding 1 litre (1¾ pints) of boiling water, 200ml (7fl oz) at a time, cooking until al dente. Remove from the heat and add the butter and Parmesan.

Mangia, ti fa bene: risotto di zucca

Death in a Strange Country, pp. 168–173

There was the smell of cooking to welcome him, one scent mingling with another. Tonight he could make out the faint odour of squash, which meant that Paola was making *risotto di zucca*, available only in this season, when the dark green, squat *barucca* squash were brought from Chioggia, across the *laguna*. And after that? Shank of veal? Roasted with olive oil and white wine?

He hung his jacket in the cupboard and went down the hall to the kitchen. The room was hotter than usual, which meant the oven was on. The large frying pan on the stove revealed, when he lifted the lid, bright orange chunks of *zucca*, frying slowly with minced onions. He took a glass from the rack beside the sink and pulled a bottle of Ribolla from the refrigerator. He poured a little more than a mouthful, tasted it, drank it down, then filled the glass and replaced the bottle. The warmth of the kitchen swept up about him. He loosened his tie and went back down the corridor. 'Paola?'

'I'm here, in the back,' he heard her answering call.

He didn't answer but went into the long living room and then out onto the balcony. This was the best time of day for Brunetti, for he could see, from their terrace, the sunset off in the West. On the clearest of days, he could see the Dolomites from the small window in the kitchen, but it was so late in the day now that they would be hazed over and invisible. He stayed where he was, forearms propped on the railing, studying the rooftops and towers that never ceased to please him. He heard Paola move down the hall, back into the kitchen, heard the clang of shifted pots, but he stayed where he was, listening to the eight o'clock bells ring out from San Polo, then to the answering resonance of San Marco, a few seconds late, as always, come booming

93

across the city. When all the bells were silent, he went back into the house, closing the door against the growing evening chill.

In the kitchen, Paola stood at the stove, stirring the risotto, pausing now and again to add more boiling broth. 'Glass of wine?' he asked. She shook her head, still stirring. He passed behind her, paused long enough to kiss her on the back of the neck, and poured himself another glass of wine.

'How was Vicenza?' she asked.

'Better to ask me how was America.'

'Yes, I know,' she said. 'It's incredible, isn't it?'

(. . .)

'It was very clean, and everyone smiled a great deal.'

'Good,' she said, stirring again. 'Then it hasn't changed.'

'I wonder why it is, that they always smile so much.' He had noticed the same thing, each time he was in America.

She turned away from the risotto and stared at him. 'Why shouldn't they smile, Guido? Think about it. They're the richest people in the world. Everyone has to defer to them in politics, and they have convinced themselves, somehow, that everything they have ever done in their very brief history has been done for no purpose other than to further the general good of mankind. Why shouldn't they smile?' She turned back to the pan and muttered darkly as she felt the rice sticking to the bottom. She poured more broth into it and stirred quickly for a moment.

'Is this going to turn into a cell meeting?' he asked blandly. Though they generally agreed about politics, Brunetti had always voted Socialist, while Paola voted, fiercely, Communist. But now, with the demise of the system and the death of the party, he had begun to take tentative shots at her.

She didn't bother to grace him with an answer.

He started to pull down plates in order to set the table. 'Where are the kids?'

'Both with friends.' Then, before he could ask, she added, 'Yes, they both called and asked permission.' She turned off the flame under the risotto, added a substantial chunk of butter that stood on the worktop, and poured in a small dish of finely grated Parmigiano Reggiano. She stirred it around until both were dissolved into the rice, poured the risotto into a serving bowl, and set it on the table. She pulled out her chair, sat down, and turned the spoon towards him, saying, '*Mangia, ti fa bene*,' a command that had filled Brunetti with joy for as long as he could remember.

He filled his dish, abundantly. He'd worked hard, spent the day in a foreign country, so who cared how much risotto he ate? Starting from the centre, he worked his fork in a neat concentric circle and pushed the risotto to the edge of his dish to help it cool faster. He took two forkfuls, sighed in appreciation, and continued to eat. (. . .)

He pulled the bowl of risotto towards him. 'Should I finish this?' he asked, not having to be a detective to know the answer.

'Go ahead. I don't like it left over, and neither do you.'

While he finished the risotto, she took the bowl from the table and placed it in the sink. He shifted two wicker mats about on the table to make a place for the roasting pan Paola took from the oven.

'What are you going to do?'

'I don't know. See what Patta does,' he said, cutting a piece of meat from the shank and placing it on her plate. With a motion of her hand, she signalled that she didn't want any more. He cut himself two large pieces, reached for some bread, and started to eat again.

COURGETTE RISOTTO WITH PRAWNS OR SHRIMPS
Risotto di zucchine con gamberoni o scampi

Serves 4

300g (11oz) prawns, shell on, or shrimps
10 tablespoons extra virgin olive oil
50g (2oz) onion, finely chopped
1 teaspoon salt
350g (12oz) courgettes, sliced into rounds
2 teaspoons crushed meat stock cube
320g (11½oz) risotto rice, e.g. Carnaroli, Arborio, Vialone Nano
1 garlic clove, finely chopped
a handful of fresh parsley, finely chopped
freshly ground black pepper

Shell the prawns, wash them and cut in half lengthways. Remove the
dark thread along the back and set aside, covered. Heat 5 tablespoons
of oil in a large non-stick pan or casserole and fry the onion lightly
with 1 teaspoon of salt and 2 tablespoons of water. When the onion is

transparent add the courgettes, 200ml (7fl oz) of water and the crushed stock cube. Mix and cook, covered, over medium heat for 15 minutes. When the mixture has been reduced, add the rice and stir in. Cook for 20–30 minutes until al dente, adding 1 litre (1¾ pints) of hot water 200ml (7fl oz) at a time. While the rice is cooking, heat the remaining oil in a frying pan and brown the garlic lightly. Add the prawns and a pinch of salt. Cook for 5 minutes, then add the parsley. Stir the prawns into the cooked rice, add a grind of pepper and serve.

Risotto with Celery and Leeks
Risotto con sedano e porro

Serves 4

8 tablespoons extra virgin olive oil

300g (11oz) green celery hearts, finely chopped

200g (7oz) leeks, white parts only, thinly sliced

1 teaspoon salt

2 teaspoons crushed meat stock cube

320g (11½oz) risotto rice, e.g. Carnaroli, Arborio, Vialone Nano

20g (¾oz) butter

30g (1oz) Parmesan cheese, grated

freshly ground black pepper

Heat the oil in a non-stick pan or casserole and add the celery and leeks along with the salt and 600ml (1 pint) of water. Cook over a medium heat for 20 minutes, stirring and gradually adding hot water until al dente. Stir the crushed stock cube into the mixture and when the vegetables are cooked dry, add the rice and stir. Cook, stirring continually and adding more hot water until the rice is soft. Remove from the heat, add the butter and cheese and mix well. Finally, add a good grind of pepper and serve.

After the summer holidays: *Risotto con sedano e porro*

Suffer the Little Children, pp. 228–229

'Would you like a glass of wine?' he asked.

'Yes. And then we can have dinner.'

He took her hand and kissed it again by way of thanks. 'White or red?' he asked.

She chose white, probably because of the risotto with leeks, which started the meal. The children had recently gone back to school, so they spent much of the meal reporting on what their classmates had done during the summer. One girl in Chiara's class had spent two months in Australia and returned disgruntled that she had traded summer for winter and then returned to autumn. Another had worked at an ice-cream shop on the island of Santorini and came back with a passable knowledge of spoken German. Raffi's best friend had backpacked from Newfoundland to Vancouver, though the quotation marks with which Raffi pronounced 'backpacked' was rich with a suggestion of trains and aeroplanes.

Brunetti did his best to follow the talk that swirled above the table, but he found himself constantly distracted by the sight of them, assailed by an overwhelming sense of possession: these were his children. Part of him was in them, the part that would go on into their children, and then into the next generation. Try as he might, however, he could recognize little of his physical self in them: only Paola seemed to have been copied. There was her nose, there the texture of her hair and that unruly curl just behind her left ear. As she spoke, Chiara waved a hand to dismiss something that had been said to her, and the gesture was Paola's.

The next course was *orata* with lemon, further reason to justify the choice of white wine. Brunetti began eating, but halfway through his portion, his attention was drawn again to Chiara, who was now in full denunciation of her English teacher.

'The subjunctive? Do you know what she told me when I asked about it?' Chiara demanded, voice rich with remembered astonishment as she glanced round the table to see that the others were prepared to respond in similar vein. When she had their attention, she said, 'That we'd get to it next year.' The noise with which she set down her fork gave ample expression of her disapproval.

RICE WITH PEAS
Risi e bisi

Serves 4
6 tablespoons extra virgin olive oil
50g (2oz) onion, finely chopped
1 teaspoon salt
350g (12oz) frozen peas
a pinch of finely chopped fresh parsley
2 teaspoons crushed meat stock cube
320g (11½oz) risotto rice, e.g. Carnaroli, Arborio, Vialone Nano
20g (¾oz) butter
30g (1oz) Parmesan cheese, grated
freshly ground black pepper

Heat the oil in a large non-stick pan or casserole and fry the onion gently with the salt and 2 tablespoons of water. When the onion is transparent, add the peas and cook over moderate heat for 15 minutes. Then add the parsley and the crushed stock cube. Once the mixture has been reduced, add the rice and blend in. Cook, stirring constantly and adding 1 litre (1¾ pints) of boiling hot water, 200ml (7fl oz) at a time. When ready, remove from the heat and add the butter, the cheese and a good grind of pepper.

The best thing you can do with peas: *Risi e bisi*

Friends in High Places, pp. 194–201

She was in the kitchen when he came in, seated at the table, shelling peas.

'*Risi e bisi*,' he said by way of greeting when he saw the peas, the irises held out in front of him.

Smiling at the sight of the flowers, she said, 'It's the best thing to do with new peas, isn't it, make risotto?' and raised her cheek to receive his kiss.

Kiss given, he answered, for no real reason, 'Unless you're a princess and you need them to put under your mattress.'

'I think the risotto's a better idea,' she answered. 'Would you put them in a vase while I finish these?' she asked, gesturing with one hand to the full paper bag on the table beside her.

He pulled a chair over to the cabinets, took a piece of newspaper from the table and spread it on the seat, then stepped up to reach for one of the tall vases that stood on top of one of the cabinets.

'The blue one, I think,' she said, looking up and watching him.

He stepped down, put the chair back in place, and took the vase over to the sink. 'How full?' he asked.

'About halfway. What would you like after?'

'What is there?' he asked.

'I've got that roast beef from Sunday. If you sliced it very thin, we could have that and then maybe a salad.'

'Is Chiara eating meat this week?' Spurred to it by an article about the treatment of calves, Chiara had a week ago declared that she would be a vegetarian for the rest of her life.

'You saw her eat the roast beef on Sunday, didn't you?' Paola asked.

'Ah, yes, of course,' he answered, turning to the flowers and tearing the paper from them.

'What's wrong?' she asked.

'The usual things,' he answered, holding the vase under the tap and turning on the cold water. 'We live in a fallen universe.'

She returned to her peas. 'Anyone who does either of our jobs should know that,' she answered.

Curious, he asked, 'How does it come from yours?' A policeman for twenty years, he needed no one to tell him that mankind had fallen from grace.

'You deal with moral decline. I deal with that of the mind.' She spoke in the elevated, self-mocking tone she often used when she caught herself taking her work seriously. Then she asked, 'Specifically, what's done this to you?' (…)

Brunetti considered this for a long time and then added, hoping to lighten the mood, 'But in both cases, I've always got to clean up the dirt.'

Paola said, 'You said that; I didn't.' When Brunetti made no response, she dropped the last of the peas into the bowl, and got to her feet. She walked to the counter and set the bowl down. 'Whichever it is you do, I suppose you'd prefer to do it on a full stomach,' she said.

Pasta and Beans
Pasta e fagioli

Serves 4
300g (11oz) dry beans (lamon or pinto beans)
3 tablespoons extra virgin olive oil
60g (2½oz) onion, thinly sliced
a pinch of finely chopped fresh rosemary
1 bay leaf
salt and freshly ground black pepper
2 teaspoons crushed meat stock cube
150g (5oz) ditaloni rigati
extra virgin olive oil

Soak the beans in a bowl of cold water for half an hour. Heat the oil in a pan or casserole and cook the onion with the rosemary, bay leaf and a pinch of salt for 2 minutes. Add 2 litres (3½ pints) of cold water, the washed and drained beans, and the crushed stock cube. Mix and cook, covered, over moderate heat for 3 hours, stirring from time to time. Adjust the seasoning with salt, add a bit of pepper and, if necessary, more water. The soup should be of a liquid consistency. When the beans are cooked pour some of them, without the broth, into a large mixing bowl (leaving the remainder in the casserole). Blend them by hand with a whisk or egg beater. Cook the pasta in a separate casserole, drain, and add to the blended beans along with the whole cooked beans and broth. Mix gently, heat and serve. If desired, a drizzle of olive oil and a grind of pepper can be added to each plate.

Having a dolcetto after *pasta e fagioli*

A Venetian Reckoning, pp. 51–54

The shops were still open when he reached his neighbourhood, so he went into the corner grocery store and bought four glass bottles of mineral water. In a weak moment of ecological appeasement, Brunetti had agreed to take part in his family's boycott of plastic bottles, and so he had, like the rest of them – he had to give them that – developed the habit of stopping at the store each time he passed to pick up a few bottles. He sometimes wondered if the rest of them bathed in the stuff while he wasn't there, with such rapidity did it disappear.

At the top of the fifth flight, he set the bag of bottles down on the final step and fished out his keys. From inside, he heard the radio news, no doubt bringing an eager public up to date on the Trevisan murder. He pushed open the door, set the bottles down inside, and closed the door behind him. From the kitchen, he heard a voice intone, '. . . denies all knowledge of the charges made against him and points to twenty years of faithful service to the ex-Christian Democratic Party as proof of his commitment to justice. From his cell in the Regina Coeli Prison, however, Renato Mustacci, confessed Mafia killer, still maintains that he was following the Senator's orders when he and two other men shot and killed Judge Filippo Preside and his wife, Elvira, in Palermo in May of last year.'

The solemn voice of the announcer was replaced by a song about soap powder, over which he could hear Paola talking aloud to herself, often her preferred audience. 'Filthy, lying pig. Filthy lying DC pig and all like him. "Commitment to justice. Commitment to justice."' There followed one of the more scurrilous epithets to which his wife was given, strangely enough, only when she spoke to herself.

She heard him coming down the hall and turned to him. 'Did you hear that, Guido? Did you hear that? All three of the killers have said he sent them to kill the judge, and he talks about his commitment to justice. They ought to take him out and hang him. But he's a Member of Parliament, so they can't touch him. Lock the whole lot of them up. Just put Parliament, every one of them, in prison and save us all a lot of time and trouble.'

Brunetti walked across the kitchen and stooped down to put the bottles in the low cabinet beside the refrigerator. There was only one other bottle there, though he had carried five up the day before. 'What's for lunch?' he asked.

She took a small step backwards and shot an accusing finger at his heart. 'The Republic's collapsing, and all he can think about is food,' she said, this time addressing the invisible listener who had, for more than twenty years, been a silent participant in their marriage. 'Guido, these villains will destroy us all. Perhaps they already have. And you want to know what's for lunch.'

Brunetti stopped himself from remarking that someone wearing cashmere from Burlington Arcade made not the best revolutionary and, instead, said, 'Feed me, Paola, and then I'll go back to my own commitment to justice.'

That was enough to remind her of Trevisan and, as Brunetti knew she would, Paola eagerly abandoned her philosophical fulminations for a bit of gossip. She turned off the radio and asked, 'Has he given it to you?'

Brunetti nodded as he pushed himself up from his knees. 'He observed that I had nothing much to do at the moment. The Mayor has already called, so I leave it to you to imagine the state he's in.' There was no need to provide explication of 'it' or 'he'.

As Brunetti knew she would be, Paola was diverted from considerations of political justice and rectitude. 'The story I read said nothing more than that he had been shot. On the train from Torino.'

'He had a ticket from Padua. We're trying to find out what he was doing there.'

'A woman?'

'Could be. Too early yet to say anything. What's for lunch?'

'Pasta fagioli and then cotoletta.'

'Salad?'

'Guido,' she asked with pursed lips and upraised eyes, 'when haven't we had salad with cutlets?'

Instead of answering her question, he asked, 'Is there any more of that good dolcetto?'

'I don't know. We had a bottle of it last week, didn't we?'

He muttered something and knelt back down in front of the cabinet. Behind the bottles of mineral water were three bottles of wine, all white. Getting to his feet again, he asked, 'Where's Chiara?'

'In her room. Why?'

'I want her to do me a favour.'

Paola glanced at her watch. 'It's a quarter to one, Guido. The stores will be closed.'

'Not if she goes up to Do Mori. They're open until one.'

'And you're going to ask her to go up there, just to get you a bottle of Dolcetto?'

'Three,' he said, leaving the kitchen and going down the hall towards Chiara's room. He knocked at the door and, from behind him, heard the radio turned on.

'*Avanti, Papà*,' she called out.

LENTIL SOUP WITH BACON
Zuppa di lenticchie con pancetta

Serves 4

300g (11oz) dry green lentils
2 tablespoons extra virgin olive oil
1 shallot, finely chopped
80g (3oz) bacon, finely chopped
a pinch of finely chopped fresh rosemary
2 bay leaves
1 fresh chilli, chopped
2 pinches of salt
2 teaspoons crushed meat stock cube
croutons, to serve

Wash the lentils. Heat the oil in a pan or casserole and fry the shallot and bacon gently with the fragrant herbs, the chilli and the salt. Add 1.5 litres (2½ pints) of hot water, the crushed stock cube and finally the drained lentils. Cover and cook over moderate heat for 45 minutes. Once cooked, place half the contents in a bowl and blend the remaining half by hand with a whisk or egg beater. Return the other half, set aside in the bowl, to the blended mixture and continue cooking, uncovered, for 20 minutes. Adjust the seasoning with salt, and serve the soup with croutons.

Detecting pancetta in the lentil soup

Uniform Justice, pp. 127–128

Brunetti arrived before the children did, so he opted to keep Paola company while she finished preparing the meal. As she set the table, he lifted pot lids and opened the oven, comforted to find nothing but familiar dishes: lentil soup, chicken smothered in red cabbage,* and what looked like *radicchio di Treviso*.*

'Are you bringing all of your detective skills to bear in examining that chicken?' Paola asked as she set glasses on the table.

'No, not really,' he said, closing the oven and standing upright. 'My investigation has to do with the radicchio, Signora, and whether there are perhaps traces in it of the same pancetta I detected in the lentil soup.'

'A nose as good as that,' she said, coming over and placing the tip of her finger on it, 'could effectively put an end to crime in this city.' She lifted the lid from the soup and stirred it round a bit, then said, 'You're back early.'

'I was over near San Marco and so it didn't make any sense to go back,' he said, taking a sip of mineral water. 'I went to see Signora Moro,' he began, pausing to see if Paola would react. She did not, so he went on, 'I wanted to talk to her about the hunting accident.'

'And?' Paola prodded.

Sant'Erasmo

It was not so long ago that most of the fruit and vegetables sold in Venice were carried in by boat from the island of Sant'Erasmo, which lies about four kilometres to the north-east of the main island and is today reachable in twenty minutes by boat number 13, which goes out once an hour. The stalls in the Rialto Market occasionally still name Sant'Erasmo as the source of some of the produce they sell: artichokes in the autumn, dark plums in late summer, occasionally peaches or salad. But by now the major portion of what is to be found at the Rialto is trucked to wholesalers at Piazzale Roma, then taken by boat to the Rialto, where it is unloaded and sold.

Thus the kiwis can, and usually do, come from New Zealand, the peaches from Spain, the apricots from France, and the tomatoes from just about anywhere in the country or, for that matter, in Europe or beyond. In the midst of this geographic abundance, however, Venetians still preserve the conviction that what comes from Sant'Erasmo is better.

This prejudice is understandable: the fact that the island is, in a sense, right *there*, means the produce is usually sold the day it is picked, or at most the day after. It has not sat around in warehouses after being delivered from Valencia or flown in from Sydney, nor has it been held captive in a nitrogen-rich room for months before being delivered to the market.

Curious about the island and about how much is still being grown there, and how, I asked my own fruit dealer, at whose stand I've been shopping for almost thirty years, if I could go out and have a look at their gardens. At first, she was surprised at my request, but when I explained that I was writing about Sant'Erasmo, she agreed and made a date at the *imbarcadero* of the number 13 for 12.25 the following day.

Her only admonition, after I mentioned that I was perfectly willing to work in the fields, was to bring some sort of mosquito repellent and be prepared for mud.

Both of us were on time, as was the nearly-empty number 13. On the way out, stopping at Murano and Le Vignole, we chatted about the island, and I asked all those questions journalists are supposed to ask. What percentage of the produce/food sold at Rialto comes from Sant'Erasmo? In the autumn, about 10 per cent; in the spring, as much as 30 per cent. How many inhabitants are there? About 750, 'but the average age is about seventy.' Then, with a smile that was more sad than happy, she added, 'You'll see.'

When we landed, she explained that we had to walk for about twenty minutes, a joy on an autumn day with a sky that had been washed clean by the night's rain. There was a bar at the boat landing, where sandwiches and drinks were available. A dozen people sat at small tables, and a few more sat chatting to them from boats moored at the landing; occasionally the people in the boats jumped up on to the dock to join their friends at the tables.

Graziella waved to the woman behind the counter, a cousin who had worked at the fruit stand for a few years. At the end of the street leading from the landing, we turned left. 'I have to stop at my aunt's,' she said. The city sewer pipe was being installed that day, and she was curious to see how things were progressing. Quickly, as it turned out: the workers were at the house next to her aunt's and had already dug the necessary trenches and holes.

We continued on towards her brother's house, and as we passed different patches of land, houses, or large fields of grass set off by fences or canals, she revealed how much had changed: 'Those used to be vegetable fields. That was an asparagus field. They grew salad there.'

On both sides of the asphalted road, squares and rectangles of neatly cut grass spread away from us. Occasionally there stood a tree: fig, peach, a few dried-up cherry trees. But aside from a few figs which were a bit past their best, there was no sign of fruit. I passed some fields with hillocks of artichokes just getting ready for the serious business of growing. Venetians have more kinds of artichoke than a non-Venetian has ever heard of: *canarini, castraure, bottoli,* each different in size and taste and each meant to be used in a different way: some for risotto, some to be fried, others to be boiled and soaked in olive oil. All to be praised as the best, far superior to those from other parts of Italy or, heaven forbid, other countries. The soil, the air, the temperature, the humidity: this combination produces the best of the best.

Graziella and I turned in at a gate, and were greeted by the wild honking of a dozen ducks waddling around in a fenced enclosure, among them Archimede, known for the sociability of his character. On the other side of the path was Jack, her brother's four-year-old English setter, who paced nervously in the manner of a dog who senses the imminent arrival of the hunting season. He allowed me to pat him on the head and scratch his ears, but his mind was really on other things, things that went quack and flew over the *laguna*.

Graziella introduced me to her mother, who sat on the patio in the afternoon sun and chatted with me while Graziella changed into her gardening clothes. The Signora told me that today was her daughter's birthday and that Graziella had been delivered at home by the midwife. Fifty years ago, the only way to get to the hospital had been to row there in a boat, but it took a long time to get to Venice, especially if the tide and the winds were against you. The two oldest were born at home, the last two in the hospital.

We chatted idly: she pointed to three young cats who were draped across various pieces of furniture on the other side of the patio, by the door to her son's house. We talked about the weather, the growing season, the approaching hunting season, and about how much things had changed in the years since her children were born. It wasn't the way it was, no one wanted to work the land any more, everyone wanted to be *un signore*.

Graziella emerged, long sleeves and high collar, not an inch of skin on offer except for her face, which had an oily sheen. Together, we gathered up plastic cases and stacked them in a wheelbarrow, then went back to the entrance, where stood ten or twelve plum trees, their branches leaning down to the grass under the weight of fruit. Each of us selected a tree: we went to work on it, and the mosquitoes went to work on us. Ignoring them, I started at the end of the lowest branch and began picking my way towards the trunk, the plums sun-warmed, dark, dusted by a faint grey haze.

Nothing on the farm had been sprayed with anything – 'There's no time' – but the plums were all perfect; no sign of mildew or blight, no holes made by insects. As soon as my hands were filled, I set the plums into the case, turning back to the same branch for more. Soon I was able to ignore the mosquitoes, who seemed intent only on buzzing and not on dining.

As the cases filled, Graziella told me what it was like to grow up on the island, knowing just about everyone, living simply and happy with that. Then, she said – as we finished the fourth case – there came the flood. She climbed down from the ladder that rested against one of the trees and pointed to a building that stood near the gate. 'See that door?' she asked. 'The water came to the top.' The water that had devastated Venice in the autumn of 1966 had done the same to Sant'Erasmo. It came sooner and stayed longer than it did in Venice, and what it rested on, this salt water, was not the pavements of a city but the earth of a farming community, where most of the people, most of the families, depended on growing crops for their survival. It spread across the land, carrying off animals and equipment, for two days, leaving behind salt-soaked fields.

'Things were bad after that,' she explained bleakly, and I was embarrassed never to have considered what the flood must have done to the islands. In a certain sense, the same flood that effectively destroyed so much of Venice's past also destroyed Sant'Erasmo's future, at least for the next few years, until the rain leached the salt from the fields. Her father went to work in a glass factory, and life changed for the family.

By then, we had filled ten cases with plums and walked down to another field, a flat mess of tomato plants that had already been picked over once. We were to pick through what was left and fill another ten cases with tomatoes that would be sold for sauce. This took two hours. The field was muddy, and many of the tomatoes were rotten. The mosquitoes here had other ideas about what to do to humans. Conversation petered out, and I began to count the cases we filled.

When there were ten of them, we left them at the side of the field to be collected later and walked back towards the house, passing Graziella's brother, who was busy hoeing away the weeds in an enormous field of lettuce. No herbicides, only the hoe and a lot of time. Luckily, perhaps because the earth here was exposed to the sun and hence dry, the mosquitoes had apparently signed a non-aggression pact.

Back at the house, after we washed, there was cake and coffee and a great deal of mineral water. And idle chat with Graziella and her mother. Yes, the population got older and older, and young people had little interest in a life that had them out of bed at four in the morning, at the Rialto Market an hour later to set things up, behind the counter until one, dismantling things, cleaning up, getting on the boat, going home to eat, and then back out into the fields to pick for the next day.

More and more people took the option of selling their fields to people from Venice who wanted a place to come to in the summer. So more and more fields were transformed into lawns, and grass replaced lettuce and artichokes. Trees were cut down and replaced by villas. As the local population continued to age and retire, farming became a hobby instead of a vocation, and young people moved away in search of work and a more exciting life.

I left at about six, walking quickly to catch the boat back to Venice. The woman at the kiosk remembered me from the vegetable stand and refused to let me pay for the glass of mineral water she gave me.

On the boat, tourists, their faces burnt by the sun, pointed at the passing islands. At Vignole, a woman with a large dog of indeterminate parentage got on, it too thrilled at the approach of hunting season, though the only thing its immediate ancestors had ever hunted was a dog biscuit.

At Fondamenta Nuove, everyone got off, tired and sun battered. I walked home, carrying a bag of tomatoes and a bag of plums. A workman is worthy of her hire.

In June, Graziella's brother closed the stand at Rialto and went to work for a Frenchman who is starting to grow wine grapes on Sant'Erasmo.

Vegetables · *Verdure*

Vegetables are beautiful as flowers.

To find them at their burgeoning best we need to go to the Rialto market, where there are stalls overflowing with vegetables of every shape and size: broccoli, cauliflower, Savoy cabbages, artichokes, aubergines of a thousand shades, and tomatoes from anywhere and everywhere. It's wonderful to wander around and see it all before choosing whatever looks tastiest. In the meantime we have the pleasure of running into friends and family, including elderly aunties who will recommend the freshest vegetables, above all those coming from . . .

. . . San Erasmo, of course!

Roberta Pianaro

VEGETABLES
Verdure

AUBERGINE AND PROSCIUTTO ROULADES
Involtini di melanzane al prosciutto

Serves 4
2–3 aubergines about 15cm/6 inches long
salt
extra virgin olive oil
12 slices oven-baked prosciutto
100g (3½oz) Emmenthal or fontina cheese
20g (¾oz) Parmesan cheese, grated

Cut the aubergines lengthways into 12 slices about 1.5cm (½ inch) thick, discarding the tough ends. Grill them, a few at a time, sprinkling a bit of salt on each slice to make them tastier and softer. Place them on a plate, drizzle with olive oil and leave to cool. To prepare the roulades, cover each aubergine slice with one slice of prosciutto. Place the cheese, divided into 12 portions and cut into strips, in the centre of each slice and roll up. Arrange the roulades side by side in an ovenproof dish. Place in a hot oven and bake at 240°C/475°F/Gas 9 for 15 minutes. Remove from the oven, discard any liquid that may have come out of the aubergines during cooking, and sprinkle with the Parmesan. Return to the oven for a few more minutes before serving.

BELGIAN ENDIVE AND SPECK ROULADES
Involtini di indivia belga allo speck

Serves 4
4 medium-sized Belgian endives
salt
80g (3oz) Emmenthal cheese
12 thin slices of speck

Wash the endives and cut each tuft in half lengthways. Place them in a large non-stick pan and sprinkle them with salt. Grill them over high heat, turning often, for about 15 minutes. Remove them from the heat, cover and cool. Re-form the original 4 tufts, placing a portion of the cheese in the middle of each one. Roll these up, using 3 slices of speck to wrap around each roll. Arrange them in an ovenproof dish, place in the oven and bake at a high temperature for around 15 minutes. Remove from the oven and discard any liquid in the bottom of the dish. Serve very hot.

Courgettes with Garlic and Parsley
Zucchine trifolate

Serves 4

800g (1¾lb) courgettes
6 tablespoons extra virgin olive oil
100g (3½oz) onion, finely chopped
1 teaspoon salt
a handful of fresh parsley, finely chopped
freshly ground black pepper

Cut the courgettes lengthways and then into slices. Heat the oil in a non-stick casserole and fry the onion lightly with the salt, adding 3 tablespoons of water. When the onion is transparent, add the courgettes. Cover and cook over a high heat for 10 minutes, stirring to avoid burning. Remove the cover and add the parsley. Lower the heat and continue cooking for 10 minutes, adding hot water if needed. When cooking is finished, only the oil should appear at the bottom of the casserole. Add a good grind of pepper and serve.

This is an excellent accompaniment for meat and fish.

The lightest part of the special meal Paola cooks when she doesn't go to the university: *zucchine trifolate*

Friends in High Places, pp. 44–45

On Fridays Paola did not have to go to the university, and so she usually spent the afternoon preparing a special meal. All of the family had come to expect it, and that night they were not disappointed. She had found a leg of lamb* at the butcher's behind the vegetable market and served it with tiny potatoes sprinkled with rosemary, *zucchine trifolate*, and baby carrots cooked in a sauce so sweet that Brunetti could have continued to eat them for dessert, had that not been pears baked in white wine.*

After dinner he lay, not unlike a beached whale, in his usual place on the sofa, permitting himself just the smallest glass of Armagnac, merely a whisper of liquid in a glass so small as barely to exist.

When Paola joined him after dismissing the children to their homework with the life-endangering threats they had come to anticipate, she sat down and, far more honest in these things than he, poured herself a healthy swig of Armagnac. 'Lord, this is good,' she said after the first sip.

COURGETTES WITH RICOTTA
Zucchine alla ricotta

Serves 4
6 courgettes, trimmed
salt
50g (2oz) Parmesan cheese, grated
250g (9oz) fresh ricotta cheese
extra virgin olive oil

Plunge the whole courgettes into a pan of boiling salted water. After about 15 minutes, when they are cooked al dente, drain them and leave to cool. Mix the Parmesan and the ricotta in a bowl. Cut the courgettes in half lengthways, scooping out the soft middle part with a paring knife. Drizzle with olive oil and sprinkle with a pinch of salt. Arrange the courgettes side by side in an ovenproof dish and place some of the cheese mixture in the centre of each. Place in a very hot oven, cook until golden and bubbling, about 10–15 minutes, and serve.

Artichokes Stuffed with Prosciutto
Carciofi ripieni al prosciutto

Serves 4

8 medium-sized globe artichokes
140g (4¾oz) oven-baked prosciutto
2 hard-boiled eggs
40g (1½oz) Parmesan cheese, grated
1 lemon
8 tablespoons extra virgin olive oil
2 teaspoons salt
2 garlic cloves, halved

Discard the tough leaves from the artichokes, trim the leaf tips, and peel the stems. Place them immediately in water with the juice of the lemon to avoid discoloration. Then drain and put them into a non-stick pan or casserole with the oil, salt, garlic and 500ml (18fl oz) of water. Cook, covered, over moderate heat for 30 minutes, then remove the lid and reduce so that only the oil is left at the bottom of the pan. Discard the garlic and leave to cool. Remove the stems along with the chokes, and with a sharp paring knife cut out the insides of the stems and place in a bowl for the stuffing. Add to this the chopped prosciutto, shelled eggs and the oil used in cooking. Mince finely with a mixer and add the Parmesan. Fill the artichokes with the mixture, heaping it up to form a dome, and arrange them upright, side by side, in an ovenproof dish, trimming the bottoms if necessary. Place in the oven and cook for 20 minutes at 180ºC/350ºF/Gas 4. Serve hot.

Cicheti in the bar: Brunetti chose artichokes

Suffer the Little Children, pp. 263–264

Brunetti stopped in a trattoria at the foot of the second bridge between the hospital and Campo Santa Marina but, finding that there was no table free, contented himself with a glass of *vino novello* and a plate of cicchetti, standing at the bar to eat them. Conversation swirled around him, but he overheard none of it, still recalling Pedrolli's surprise when asked about his medical records, or had it been at the suggestion that inappropriate use might have been made of them?

The *fondi di carciofi* were delicious, and Brunetti asked for two more, then another *polpetta* and another glass of wine. When he was finished, he was still not satisfied, though he was no longer hungry. These pick-up meals that he was often forced to eat were one of the worst things about his job, along with the too-frequent early morning calls, such as the one that had begun this story for him. He paid and left, cut behind the Miracoli and down towards Campo Santa Marina.

ARTICHOKES COOKED IN A CASSEROLE
Carciofi in casseruola

Serves 4
8 medium-sized globe artichokes
½ a lemon
6 tablespoons extra virgin olive oil
1 teaspoon salt
1 garlic clove, halved
a handful of parsley, finely chopped
freshly ground black pepper

Cut off the artichoke stems and peel. Remove all the tough leaves from the artichokes and trim the tips thoroughly. Place them immediately in a bowl of cold water with the lemon juice to prevent discoloration. Wash and drain the artichokes and arrange side by side in a non-stick pan or casserole with the stems, oil, salt, garlic, and 750ml (1¼ pints) of water. Cover and place over a high heat. When the water comes to the boil, add the parsley and cook for 30 minutes. Remove the cover, lower the heat and boil off the remaining water so that only the oil is left at the bottom of the pan. Remove from the heat, and add a grind of pepper and arrange on a serving platter. Serve hot or cold – both are good!

WHITE CAULIFLOWER WITH BÉCHAMEL
Cavolfiore bianco con besciamella

Serves 4
1kg (2¼lb) white cauliflower
salt
20g (¾oz) butter
120g (4oz) Emmenthal cheese, cut in small cubes

For the béchamel sauce
50g (2oz) butter
50g (2oz) very fine flour
1 teaspoon or more salt
500ml (18fl oz) hot milk
a grind of nutmeg

Plunge the cauliflower into a large pan of boiling salted water and cook for around 15 minutes or until al dente. Drain, cut into medium-sized pieces and set aside. Place the butter for the béchamel sauce in a non-stick pan and melt. Blend in the flour and salt, using a wooden spoon, to obtain a cream. Remove from the heat and add the milk, stirring constantly with a whisk until smooth. Return to the heat and thicken the sauce, still stirring. Add a grind of nutmeg at the end. Place the butter in small pieces at the bottom of an ovenproof dish, add the cauliflower, sprinkle with the Emmenthal and cover with the béchamel sauce. Place in a hot oven for about 20 minutes, or until the béchamel is a nice golden colour. Serve, though not too hot.

LATE TREVISO RADICCHIO WITH STRACCHINO
Radicchio tardivo di Treviso con Stracchino

Serves 4
800g (1¾lb) heads of radicchio
salt
extra virgin olive oil
freshly ground black pepper
130g (4½oz) stracchino cheese (or any other soft, runny cheese)

Remove any damaged leaves from the radicchio. Wash them whole, drain, and cut them lengthways in 4 or 6 segments according to their thickness. Place them in a very large preheated non-stick frying pan and cook, turning often, until wilted. Add a pinch of salt, remove from the heat and leave to stand, covered for 30 minutes. Then arrange them side by side on a baking sheet, drizzle with oil, add a grind of pepper and place the cheese, cut into small pieces, on top. Place in a hot oven and bake at maximum temperature for at least 15 minutes, or until the cheese has melted. Remove from the oven and serve.

One of the delights of early winter: smothered radicchio

Blood from a Stone, pp. 32–36

Up until that point, dinner had been a normal enough affair, at least as normal as a meal can be when it has been delayed by murder. Brunetti, who had been called from home only minutes before they sat down, had phoned a little after nine, saying he would still be some time. The children's complaints that they were on the verge of expiring from hunger had by then worn down Paola's resistance, so she fed them, putting her own dinner and Guido's back in the oven to keep warm. She sat with the children, sipping idly from a glass of prosecco that gradually grew warm and flat as the children ate their way through enormous portions of a pasticcio made of layers of polenta, ragù, and parmigiano. To follow there was only roasted radicchio smothered in stracchino, though Paola marvelled that either one of her children could possibly eat anything else.

'Why's he always have to be late?' Chiara complained as she reached for the radicchio.

'He's not always late,' a literal-minded Paola answered.

'It seems that way,' Chiara said, selecting two long stalks and lifting them on to her plate, then carefully spooning melted cheese on top.

'He said he'd be here as soon as he could.'

'It's not like it's so important or anything, is it? That he has to be so late?' Chiara asked.

Paola had explained the reason for their father's absence, and so she found Chiara's remark not a little strange.

'I thought I told you someone was killed,' she said mildly.

'Yes, but it was only a *vu cumprà*,' Chiara said as she picked up her knife.

It was at this remark that Paola's mouth fell open. She picked up her

134

glass of wine, pretended to take a sip, moved the platter of radicchio towards Raffi, who appeared not to have heard his sister, and asked, 'What do you mean by, "only", Chiara?' Her voice, she was glad to note, was entirely conversational.

'Just what I said, that it wasn't one of us,' her daughter answered.

Paola tried to identify sarcasm or some attempt to provoke her in Chiara's response, but there was no hint of either. Chiara's tone, in fact, seemed to echo her own in terms of calm dispassion.

'By "us", do you mean Italians or all white people, Chiara?' she asked.

'No,' Chiara said, 'Europeans.'

'Ah, of course,' Paola answered, picking up her glass and toying with the stem for a moment before setting it down, untested. 'And where are the borders of Europe?' she finally asked.

'What, *Mamma*?' asked Chiara, who had been answering a question put to her by Raffi. 'I didn't hear you.'

'I asked where the borders of Europe were.'

'Oh, you know that, *Mamma*. It's in all the books.' Before Paola could say anything, Chiara asked, 'Is there any dessert?'

As a young mother, Paola, herself an only child and without any previous experience of small children, had read all the books and manuals that gave modern parents advice on how to treat their children. She had, further, read many books of psychology, and knew that there was a general professional consensus that one should never subject a child to severe criticism until the reasons for their behaviour or words had been explored and examined, and even then, the parent was enjoined to take into consideration the possibility of damaging the developing psyche of the child.

'That's the most disgusting, heartless thing I've ever heard said at this table, and I am ashamed to have raised a child capable of saying it,' she said.

Raffi, who had tuned in only when his radar registered his mother's tone, dropped his fork. Chiara's mouth fell open in a mirror of her mother's expression, and for much the same reason: shock and horror that a person so fundamental to her happiness could be capable of such a speech. Like her mother, she dismissed even the possibility of diplomacy and demanded, 'What's that supposed to mean?'

'It's supposed to mean that *vu cumpràs* are not *only* anything. You can't dismiss them as if their deaths don't matter.'

Chiara heard her mother's words; more significantly, she felt the force of her mother's tone, and so she said, 'That's not what I meant.'

'I've no idea what you meant, Chiara, but what you *said* was that the dead man was *only* a *vu cumprà*. And you'd have to do a lot of explaining to make me believe that there's any difference between what those words *say* and what they *mean*.'

Chiara set her fork down on her plate and asked, 'May I go to my room?'

Raffi, his own fork motionless in his hand, turned his head back and forth between them, confused that Chiara had said what she did and stunned by the power of his mother's response.

'Yes,' Paola said.

Chiara stood, quietly pushed her chair back under the table, and left the room. Raffi, who was familiar with his mother's sense of humour, turned to her, waiting for the one-line remark he was sure would come. Instead, Paola got to her feet and picked up her daughter's plate. She placed it in the sink, then went into the living room.

Raffi finished his radicchio, resigned himself to the fact that there would be no dessert that night, set his knife and fork neatly parallel on his plate, then took it over to the sink. He went back to his room.

BAKED STUFFED TOMATOES
Pomodori ripieni al forno

Serves 4

8 medium round tomatoes
5 slices of bread, without crusts
4 tablespoons extra virgin olive oil
1 teaspoon salt
1 medium egg, beaten
1 garlic clove, crushed
50g (2oz) Parmesan cheese, grated

Wash and dry the tomatoes, slicing off the tops. With a fine-edged paring knife, scoop out the insides, liquid and seeds included, into a bowl. Place the bread, cut into pieces, in a mixing bowl and soak with the tomato liquid (but not the seeds, so put it through a sieve). Add the oil, salt, egg and garlic and mix together to form a fairly thick cream. Finally, add the cheese. Dry the insides of the tomatoes well and salt them lightly. Fill them with the creamy sauce, finishing just above the top edge to form a small dome. Arrange them on a baking sheet lined with baking parchment. Place in a hot oven and bake for about 20 minutes, then turn off the oven and leave the tomatoes to rest inside for another 5 minutes. Remove from the oven, arrange on a plate and serve.

Spring Vegetable Stew
Primavera di verdure

Serves 4

2 aubergines
3 large ripe tomatoes
1 red pepper
1 yellow pepper
2 courgettes
2 white onions
1 hot fresh chilli
1 teaspoon salt
8 tablespoons extra virgin olive oil
50ml (2fl oz) dry white wine
a sprig of fresh parsley, finely chopped
1 garlic clove, crushed
60g (2½oz) dried black olives, stoned and chopped

First prepare the vegetables. Use only the skins of the aubergines, cut lengthways in a thickness of about 1cm (1/3 inch), then into strips. Peel the tomatoes and cut them into chunks. Cut the peppers into pieces, slice the courgettes, and thinly slice the onions. Place all the vegetables in a large non-stick casserole with the chilli, salt and oil. Cook over high heat for 20 minutes, stirring often. Add the wine, parsley, garlic and olives. Stir and cook until only the oil remains at the bottom of the casserole.

This vegetable blend is excellent with any kind of pasta.

Potatoes with Cream
Patate alla panna

Serves 4
1kg (2¼lb) potatoes
salt
butter
250ml (8fl oz) fresh cream

Cook the potatoes in their skins in boiling salted water, then drain and leave to cool. Peel them and slice into rounds. Arrange side by side in a buttered ovenproof dish, sprinkle with a pinch of salt and pour over the cream. Place in a hot oven and bake until the cream thickens and browns on the surface.

A vegetable accompaniment for oven-baked fish dishes.

Savoury Carrots
Carote gustose

Serves 4
500g (1lb 2oz) carrots, sliced
500g (1lb 2oz) ripe tomatoes, roughly chopped
400g (14oz) leeks, white part only, thinly sliced
1 teaspoon salt
6 tablespoons extra virgin olive oil
50g (2oz) raisins, washed and pressed
1 tablespoon grated fresh root ginger

Place the vegetables in a non-stick pan or casserole with 4 tablespoons of oil and a teaspoon of salt. Cover and cook over moderate heat for 20 minutes, stirring from time to time. Remove the cover and add the raisins, the ginger, and the remaining 2 tablespoons of oil. Switch off the oven and leave to season for another few minutes, then serve.

Capitano Alberto

In a cookbook, especially one featuring Venetian food, one must write about fish, but to do that one needs a fisherman, someone who has spent his life catching and eating them. I spent some time asking friends who would be best suited to talk to me about fish, and most of them agreed that it would be Capitano Alberto, a man with salt water in his veins, a man who knows more about the *laguna* and what is swimming in its waters and clinging to its bottom than anyone else in the city.

He proved, as Italians so often are, *disponibilissimo* to my request, and we met in front of the church of San Pietro di Castello because he and his wife have the good fortune to live in one of the apartments in the convent. Alberto is . . . well, he is *robusto*. In some other language, such a word might suggest that he is fat, but this is not the case, not at all. He's not particularly tall, but he is broad, and there is evidence that he has done, as he later said, '*onore alla tavola*'. Much honour and many tables, I'm sure, but still his bulk emanates energy and strength, and there is no trace of the lethargy common to so many of those who are overweight.

Six generations ago, a Turkish ancestor of his was brought to Venice as a prisoner of war: over time they ceased being Turks, didn't bother wasting time becoming Italians, and were transformed directly into Venetians, though Alberto says he does not feel Venetian so much as he does a person who lives in Castello, specifically in San Pietro di Castello.

I think anyone would know instantly that Alberto is a man of the sea. His white hair is cut short, his eyes are the blue of shallow sea water, his nose is important to his face. The skin on that face has been tanned and re-tanned and then tanned again by years on the decks and at the helm of the boats, large and small, that he has worked on and captained. When we met, I had the fleeting impression that I had already met him, but Venice is a city on the sea, and he is a common nautical type, and so I dismissed the idea.

Born in Castello, Alberto can't remember a time when he did not know how to swim, and was first involved in commercial fishing when he was ten and started to catch razor clams to sell to *trattorie*. At sixteen, he sold the family library and bought himself a mask so he could fish underwater with an air rifle, and at twenty he began to fish with nets. He showed me the barrels where he still keeps the nets he has woven, carefully pointing out that the mesh was sufficiently large to allow small fish to escape. Unlike many of today's commercial fishermen, Capitano Alberto thinks far into the future and realizes the importance of catching only adult fish and letting the little ones go. 'So they can grow up,' he explains. 'Leave something for our children to eat.'

He described what it was like to fish back in his youth and middle years thirty, forty years ago: navigating entirely by the stars; forecasting the weather by experience, not by instruments; sleeping through the winter nights rolled up beneath the prow with only a blanket between him and the damp and the cold; waiting, praying for the first sight of the sun and the lambent glow on the horizon that brought back light and warmth.

With visible emotion, he spoke of a friend with whom he had fished, a man, like him, born to the sea, who had died decades earlier. He spoke of the bond that develops when men, alone in a boat for nights on end, open their hearts to one another, forging a bond closer than a man has with his father. When this friend died, Alberto's wife, then fifty, took his place on the boat, the only woman in Italy at that time who had a fishing licence. 'She's the best sailor I ever had.'

In the 1970s, when his wife was pregnant with their first daughter, she woke up one morning, stepped out of bed and put her feet . . . into water. They lived on the ground floor, and *acqua alta* had slipped into the city – and into their apartment – during the night. Frightened for her health, Alberto, who was then working for the railway, accepted his employer's offer of a free apartment in the city of Mestre: large, warm, and filled with light. They moved to Mestre, these people who had been Venetian for generations, and found themselves surrounded by cars, traffic, bicycles, no sign of the sea, and endless noise.

They remained silent, each of them convinced that the other was happy with this lovely, warm home, until the baby was born, when one of them broke down and revealed how '*Questa Mestre mi sta sulle palle*' – 'Mestre busts my balls.' The words were no sooner out than Alberto walked across the street and spoke to a man who owned a truck, and that very day – rather in the manner of Mary and Joseph and the baby Jesus – they fled the city and returned to San Pietro di Castello, into the apartment where they still live, and where there are no cars, no traffic, no bicycles, no noise, and where they can see salt water from their windows.

As we spoke, the feeling that I'd already known this man grew stronger. We had friends in common, but I knew I had never been out on a boat with him, knew we had never had a meal together. Yet the sensation remained that we had somehow done something together, shared some vital experience.

I turned the topic to cooking and eating fish, hoping for advice from the expert. 'It's not important what fish you eat,' he told me. 'It's important only that the fish be fresh.' He smiled, seeing my hesitation. 'When I eat fish, I know where it's come from, what part of the *laguna*. I can tell if what I'm eating is a wild fish or a factory fish.' He said these last words the way another person might say 'garbage'.

Then, as if wanting to show his credentials as something other than a fisherman, he mentioned the navigational licences he had earned and ships he had commanded. Nor did he want me to think of him as an untutored man: we spoke of the books we'd read and the writers we admired. His favorite is Kafka, who 'drew a sketch in which people could see themselves'. He smiled, not a happy smile, and added, 'He is my joy and my damnation. After reading Kafka, no author has salt for me.'

He mentioned other authors, chiefly the English captains and explorers of previous ages who had written about their voyages –

Anson, Cook, Conrad – and some writers I'd heard of but never read.

And then I remembered. 'Capitano,' I asked, 'have you read the novels of Patrick O'Brian?'

'Of course.'

It returned to me then, a brief conversation I had had in a hardware store, at least ten years earlier, with a robust man with a sea-seared face, who had been speaking to the salesman of the novels of *Paddreek O'Breeon*, with whose novels he was enchanted. I'd spoken up then, telling him that I too shared a passion for the novels of Patrick O'Brian, and he had won my reader's heart by telling me how much he envied me, 'Because they are all written in English, all of them – and so you can read them all – but only seven have been translated into Italian.' And here he was, a decade later, still enchanted with the sea and with books about the sea. In the midst of glory, ordinary life plods along.

Our talk moved away from books when I asked him to explain the fishing year to me, which he quickly did. In January and February it is generally too cold to fish. In March, however, the cuttlefish begin to come closer to the coast in order to lay their eggs, and if he manages to catch enough of them, a fisherman can lay aside enough money to serve as a financial cushion for the rest of the season.

May and June bring in the *squalletti*, the small sharks that Venetians call *cagnoletti*, 'little dogs', which are best cooked in tomato sauce and eaten with polenta. The heat of the summer brings *soglie* and all the varied types of *cefali*.

The autumn brings abundance in the form of the fish that have been living and eating well in the *laguna* all summer and which are consequently heavier and better tasting than those who have been on short rations in the Adriatic. This is when the fisherman brings in the prize fish: sole, branzino (sea bass), orate, triglie.

His explanation of the fishing year complete, Alberto moved on to a condemnation of current fishing practices, especially of the *vongolari* who go out at night and dredge the bottom of the *laguna* for clams, careless of what else they destroy as they drag their metal sieves along the seabed, leaving destruction in their wake. The clams they harvest illegally, hundreds of kilos in a night, are almost all descended from clams imported from the Philippines and planted on the seabed where, because they have no natural predators, they have successfully overcome the native species. It's easy enough for the illegal fishermen to dispose of them: accomplices in cars and trucks have to do nothing more than drive to a convenient meeting point somewhere along the coast and unload the clams, after which they can easily be sold. I asked him about the difference in taste between Venetian and Philippine clams, and he dismissed the possibility of comparison with a single wave of his thick hand.

About the general fate of fishing and fish, Captain Alberto is pessimistic: he referred to a Venetian law of 1753 which declared that all fish had to be auctioned – live – at San Marco, and so the fish were brought there in boats with wells in the middle to keep them alive until they were sold. Today, instead, fish are caught in nets that trail kilometres behind the boats, and as much is tossed away as is kept. What is sold is often kept frozen for months, sometimes defrosted and refrozen during that time, and some of it is sold along with fish grown in enormous farms that produce the equivalent of battery chickens.

I was curious about the fish at the Rialto Market, all of which must now, by European law, carry the fish equivalent of a passport that declares where they come from and whether they have been frozen or not. Some of them come thousands of kilometres to get to market: they do not come by swimming.

'What fish do you eat, Capitano?'

'Any fish I catch.'

'And Rialto, would you buy fish there?'

He hesitated for an instant. 'If I know the man selling it,' he said, and smiled. 'It's enough that a fish be fresh,' he told me again. 'It doesn't matter what kind of fish it is. You can tell by the eye, you can tell by the scales, you can tell by the smell.' I wished there had been a fish on the table between us so that he could have shown me, but there were only empty coffee cups.

'Fish has to be fresh. Factory fish are like women today: plastic tits, everything smelling of *detersivo*. All the same.'

'And cooking it, and eating it?' I asked, remembering what my original intention had been.

'All fish needs is to be cooked on the grill with a little salt. If it's fresh, that's enough.'

'Should you add anything to flavour it?' I asked, thinking of the fish I'd eaten and the recipes I'd read.

'Let me tell you an old saying,' he said by way of answer:

'Chi nel pesce mette limone,
E' un gran coglione.'

Roughly, this means only idiots put lemon on fish. So that's it, gentle reader: fresh fish on the grill – doesn't much matter what kind of fish so long as it's fresh, served with a bit of salt, and no lemon. Captain's order.

Fish and Seafood · *Pesci e frutti di mare*

Although we're at the market to buy vegetables, why not also have a look at the fish? As we walk around, a whole universe of fish in myriad shapes and colours opens before our eyes: giltheads that come only from the valleys of the lagoon, their shiny scales shining in the light; speckled turbot from the northern Adriatic; strange-looking John Dory from the Atlantic; soft red scorpion fish from the Mediterranean, with their swollen bellies. A huge one-eyed cuttlefish captivates us with its beautiful patterning, while the little grey shrimps, still alive and jumping, risk ending up squashed on the ground below by the passing crowds.

The show is always exciting, even if we've seen it hundreds of times before, and we never get tired of sampling a particular fish or shellfish, cooked just the way we like it.

Eventually we choose a counter to stop at. Amid the various demands for freshness and reassurances of quality, we catch the eye of the person next to us and enjoy a moment of tacit understanding,

before sharing our impressions of today's market, past experiences and precious advice on the best way to cook our chosen dish.

Finally, we make our way home with our prey in the little bag that's a bit cold and a bit damp, just as though it had been handed to us by the fishermen themselves.

Roberta Pianaro

FISH AND SEAFOOD
Pesci e frutti di mare

Monkfish with tomatoes   155
Code di rospo al pomodoro

Monkfish cutlets with peppers   159
Cotolette di coda di rospo ai peperoni

Boiled grey mullet with green olive mayonnaise   161
'Bosega': cefalo volpina bollita con maionese alle olive verdi

Sole with artichoke hearts and rocket   163
Sogliole con cuori di carciofo e rucola

Swordfish with savoury breadcrumbs   166
Pesce spada al pangrattato saporito

Turbot fillets with leeks, capers and raisins   167
Filetti di rombo con porri, capperi, uvetta

Salmon fillets cooked with mushrooms and scented with basil   169
Filetti di salmone ai funghi, profumati al basilico

Baked sea bass   170
Branzino al forno

Stuffed squid with tomato sauce   172
Calamari ripieni al sugo di pomodoro

Stewed black cuttlefish   176
Seppie nere in umido

Monkfish with Tomatoes
Code di rospo al pomodoro

Serves 4
1.4kg (3lb) monkfish tails, each about 350g (12oz)
100g (3½oz) flour
8 tablespoons extra virgin olive oil
2 garlic cloves, finely chopped
2 teaspoons salt
a pinch of dried chilli
500g (1lb 2oz) tomatoes, peeled and chopped
a sprig of fresh parsley, finely chopped
a handful of fragrant fresh herbs (e.g. rosemary, thyme, marjoram)

Wash and dry the monkfish tails and coat them lightly with flour. Heat the oil in a large non-stick casserole and fry the garlic lightly with the salt and the chilli. Add the tomatoes and cook until the sauce thickens, then add the fish and cook for 25 minutes, turning from time to time, and adding the parsley and other herbs 5 minutes before removing from the heat. Serve very hot.

After glass, Murano's best: *coda di rospo*

Through a Glass, Darkly, pp. 95–99

Before Brunetti could answer, a waiter came to the table. He had no pen or order pad, rattled off the menu and asked them what they'd like.

Navarro said the men were friends of his, which caused the waiter to recite the menu again, slowly, with comments, even with recommendations.

They ended up asking for spaghetti with *vongole*.* The waiter winked to suggest that they had been dredged up, perhaps illegally, but definitely in the *laguna*, the night before. Brunetti had never much liked liver, so he asked for a grilled *rombo*,* while Vianello and Navarro both asked for *coda di rospo*.

'*Patate bollite?*' the waiter asked before he walked away.

They all said yes.

Without asking, the waiter was soon back with a litre of mineral water and one of white wine, which he set down on their table before going into the kitchen, where they could hear him shouting out their order.

As if there had been no interruption, Brunetti asked, 'What do you know about him? Do you work for him?'

'No,' Navarro answered, obviously surprised by the question. 'But I know him. Everyone here does. He's a bastard.' Navarro tore open a packet of *grissini*. He put one in his mouth and nibbled it right down to the bottom, like a cartoon rabbit eating a carrot.

'You mean in the sense that he's difficult to work with?' Brunetti asked.

'You said it. He's had two *maestri* now for about two years: longest he's ever kept any of them, far as I know.'

'Why is that?' asked Vianello, pouring wine for all of them.

'Because he's a bastard.' Even Navarro sensed the circularity of his argument and so added, 'He'll try on anything to cheat you.'

'Could you give us an example?' Brunetti asked.

This seemed to stump Navarro for a moment, as though a request to supply evidence to support a judgement were a novelty for him. He drank a glass of wine, filled his glass and drank another, then ate two more *grissini*. Finally he said, 'He'll always hire *garzoni* and let them go before they can become *serventi* so he won't have to pay them more. He'll keep them for a year or so, working off the books or working with two-month contracts, but then when it's time for them to move up, and get more money, he fires them. Invents some reason to get rid of them, and hires new ones.'

'How long can he go on doing this?' Vianello asked.

Navarro shrugged. 'So long as there are boys who need jobs, he can probably go on doing it for ever.'

'What else?'

'He argues and fights.'

'With?' Vianello asked.

'Suppliers, workers, the guys on the boats who bring the sand or the guys on the boats who take the glass away. If there's money involved – and there's money involved in all of this – then he'll argue with them.'

'I've heard about a fight in a bar a couple of years ago . . .' Brunetti began and let his voice drop away.

'Oh, that,' Navarro said. 'It's probably the one time the old bastard didn't start it. Some guy said something he didn't like and De Cal said something back, and the guy hit him. I wasn't there, but my brother was. Believe me, he hates De Cal more than I do, so if he said the old bastard didn't start it, then he didn't.'

'What about his daughter?' Brunetti asked.

Before Navarro could answer, the waiter brought their pasta and set the plates in front of them. Conversation stopped as the three men dug into the spaghetti. The waiter returned with three empty plates for the shells.

'Peperoncino,' Brunetti said, mouth full.

'Good, eh?' Navarro said.

Brunetti nodded, took a sip of wine, and returned to the spaghetti, which was better than good. He had to remember to tell Paola about the peperoncino, which was more than she used but still good.

When their plates were empty and the other plates full of shells, the waiter came and took them all away, asking if they had eaten well. Brunetti and Vianello said enthusiastic things: Navarro, a regular customer, was not obliged to comment.

Soon the waiter was back with a bowl of potatoes and the fish: Brunetti's was already filleted. Navarro asked for olive oil, and the waiter returned with a bottle of much better oil. All three poured it on their fish but not on the potatoes, which already sat in a pool of it at the bottom of the bowl. None of them spoke for some time.

While Vianello spooned the last of the potatoes from the bowl, Brunetti returned to his questions and asked, 'His daughter, do you know much about her?'

Monkfish Cutlets with Peppers
Cotolette di coda di rospo ai peperoni

Serves 4
700g (1½lb) monkfish fillets (8 fillets)
50g (2oz) flour
50ml (2fl oz) extra virgin olive oil
salt

For the sauce
1 red pepper
1 yellow pepper
300g (11oz) leeks
5 tablespoons extra virgin olive oil
salt and freshly ground black pepper
1 garlic clove, finely chopped
a pinch of fresh parsley, finely chopped

Open the monkfish fillets out like a book so as to obtain 8 cutlets, pounding them a bit until slightly thinner. Wash them, dry them thoroughly with kitchen paper or under the grill, and coat them with the flour. Roast the peppers over a burner to char them, then peel them and cut into thin strips lengthways. Wash the leeks and cut them first lengthways and then into thin slices. Place them in a non-stick casserole with the 5 tablespoons of oil, a pinch of salt and 200ml (7fl oz) of water. Cook for 20 minutes, stirring often, then add the pepper strips, garlic, parsley and pepper. Stir and adjust the seasoning. If necessary, reduce the mixture to remove any excess water. Heat the 50ml (2fl oz) of oil in a large non-stick frying pan and add the monkfish cutlets and a pinch of salt. Cook, turning, for 2–3 minutes. Arrange the fish side by side on a serving platter and top with the pepper sauce. Serve very hot.

Boiled Grey Mullet with Green Olive Mayonnaise

'Bosega': cefalo volpina bollita con maionese alle olive verdi

Serves 4

1 grey mullet weighing 1kg (2¼lb), gutted, scaled and cleaned (ask your fishmonger to do this for you)

1 onion

1 celery stalk

3 bay leaves

salt

whole green olives, to garnish

For the mayonnaise

1 egg yolk

100ml (3½fl oz) corn oil

1 tablespoon lemon juice

a pinch of salt

50g (2oz) green olives, stoned and chopped

Put the onion and celery into a casserole of salted water, add the bay leaves and boil, covered, for 30 minutes. Remove from the heat and leave to cool. Place the fish in the vegetable broth and simmer, covered, for 15 minutes. Remove from the heat and cool in the broth for another 15 minutes. Arrange the fillets on a serving dish.

To make the mayonnaise, place the egg yolk in a bowl and beat with a small whisk. Put the oil in a small jug and add in a drizzle, just a bit at a time, beating constantly. When the sauce has thickened, add the lemon juice, a little at a time, alternating it with the oil and continuing to beat. Finally, add the salt and the olives.

Spread the sauce carefully over the mullet and garnish with whole olives. Serve at room temperature. This is also excellent cold, as an antipasto.

Sole with Artichoke Hearts and Rocket
Sogliole con cuori di carciofo e rucola

Serves 4

4 sole fillets, about 250g (9oz) each
4 medium-sized globe artichokes
juice of ½ a lemon
10 tablespoons extra virgin olive oil
1 garlic clove, halved
salt and freshly ground black pepper
a pinch of finely chopped fresh parsley
150g (5oz) rocket
balsamic vinegar

Wash the sole fillets and pat dry with kitchen paper. Cut off the artichoke stems, remove all the tough leaves and trim the tips. Wash them and cut in half lengthways. Remove the chokes and slice the artichokes very finely, starting from the bottom. As you work, place them in a bowl and sprinkle them well with the lemon juice. Set aside for a few minutes. Heat the oil in a large non-stick pan or casserole and brown the garlic gently with some salt. Add the sliced artichokes and cook for at least 15 minutes, adding a little hot water and the parsley. When only the oil can be seen at the bottom of the casserole, add the sole fillets, side by side, season with a little more salt and cook for 5 minutes, turning once. Add a grind of pepper, remove from the heat and serve very hot, accompanied by the rocket, dressed with oil, balsamic vinegar and salt.

A prickly scene: sole with artichokes

Blood from a Stone, pp. 80–84

If he had thought to leave uncertainty and unease behind him at the Questura, he was much mistaken, for he found both within the walls of his home. Here they manifested themselves in the aura of moral outrage which both Paola and Chiara carried about with them, much in the fashion of Dante's usurers, passing through eternity with their money bags hung round their necks. He assumed that both his wife and his daughter believed themselves in the right. When, after all, had a person involved in an argument believed themselves to be in the wrong?

He found his family at table. He kissed Paola's cheek and ruffled Chiara's hair, but she pulled her head quickly aside, as if unwilling to be touched by a hand that had rested on her opponent's shoulder. Pretending not to have noticed, he took his place and asked Raffi how school was. His son, in a manifestation of male solidarity in the face of female moodiness, said things were fine, then began a long explanation of the arcane of a computer program he was using in his chemistry class. Brunetti, far more interested in

164

his linguine with scampi than in anything to do with computers, smiled and asked what he did his best to make sound like relevant questions.

Conversation chugged along through a plate of sole fried with artichoke hearts and a rucola salad. Chiara pushed her food around on her plate, leaving much of it uneaten, an unmistakable sign that this situation was affecting her deeply.

Upon learning that there was no dessert, she and Raffi evaporated; Brunetti set his empty glass down and said, 'I have the feeling I ought to have one of those blue helmets the UN peacekeepers wear when there's danger they might be caught in crossfire.'

Paola poured them both a bit more wine, the Loredan Gasparini his father-in-law had sent him as a birthday present, one he would like to be able to drink in happier circumstances. 'She'll get over it,' Paola said and set the bottle on the table with an authoritative clunk.

'I have no doubt of that,' Brunetti answered calmly. 'I just don't want to have to eat my lunch in this atmosphere until that happens.'

(…)

She pursed her lips, glanced across at the window that looked off to the north, nodded in acknowledgment of the accuracy of his question, and said, 'You're right.'

'I'm not interested in being right,' Brunetti said.

'What are you interested in, then?'

'Living in peace in my own home.'

'I suppose that's pretty much all anyone wants,' she said.

'If only it were that simple, huh?' he asked, got to his feet and leaned over to kiss her on the head, then went back to the Questura and to the investigation of the death of the man who was only a *vu cumprà*.

SWORDFISH WITH SAVOURY BREADCRUMBS
Pesce spada al pangrattato saporito

Serves 4
600g (1lb 5oz) swordfish (2 slices cut into four)
100g (3½oz) breadcrumbs, plus extra to finish
a sprig of finely chopped fresh parsley
6 tablespoons extra virgin olive oil
20g (¾oz) capers preserved in salt, washed and finely chopped
1 garlic clove, crushed
30g (1oz) Parmesan cheese, grated
2 medium eggs
a pinch of salt

Wash the swordfish and dry with kitchen paper. Place the 100g (3½ oz) of breadcrumbs in a mixing bowl with the parsley, oil, capers, garlic and cheese. Mix well. In another mixing bowl, beat the eggs with the salt. Dip each swordfish slice in the egg mixture and then into the breadcrumb blend. Arrange them side by side on a baking sheet lined with baking parchment. Cover each swordfish slice with more breadcrumbs for an even tastier result. Place in a preheated oven and bake for 20 minutes at maximum temperature.

Turbot Fillets with Leeks, Capers and Raisins
Filetti di rombo con porri, capperi, uvetta

Serves 4
600g (1lb 5oz) turbot fillet, divided into 8 pieces
10 tablespoons extra virgin olive oil
salt and freshly ground black pepper
200g (7oz) leeks, white part only, finely sliced
60g (2½oz) raisins, washed and pressed
30g (1oz) capers preserved in salt, washed and crumbled
juice of 1 lemon

Wash the turbot fillets, dry thoroughly and set aside. Heat 5 tablespoons of the oil in a large non-stick pan and add 1 teaspoon of salt and the leeks. Stir, add 200ml (7fl oz) of water and cook over moderate heat for 15 minutes, adding a little more water from time to time. The leeks must not burn. Add the raisins, capers and a good grind of pepper and continue cooking for 5 minutes or until the leeks are tender. In another large non-stick pan, heat the remaining 5 tablespoons of oil with a pinch of salt. Add the turbot fillets and cook them very lightly, turning once and adding the lemon juice. Remove them from the pan and place gently over the leeks. Let season for 2 minutes, and serve hot.

Salmon Fillets Cooked with Mushrooms and Scented with Basil
Filetti di salmone ai funghi, profumati al basilico

Serves 4
600g (1lb 5oz) wild salmon, in one piece, skinned
50g (2oz) butter
2 shallots, finely chopped
1 teaspoon salt
400g (14oz) mushrooms, stems removed, caps sliced
50ml (2fl oz) dry white wine
freshly ground black pepper
150g (5oz) fresh cream
a bunch of basil, torn into small strips

Cut the salmon slice into small pieces crossways, in a thickness of around 4cm (1½ inches). Wash and dry the fish with kitchen paper and set aside, covered. Heat 30g (1oz) of the butter in a non-stick pan and fry the shallots gently, adding the salt and a tablespoon of water to prevent burning. Add the mushrooms and cook for 15 minutes, until dry. Pour in the wine, let it evaporate, and add pepper and the fresh cream. Stir until the sauce begins to thicken, then set aside over a low heat. In another pan, heat the remaining 20g (¾oz) of butter and add the fish pieces with a pinch of salt, cooking them slightly and turning once. Remove from the heat and blend gently with the mushrooms. Let season for 2–3 minutes, then add the basil, and serve hot.

BAKED SEA BASS
Branzino al forno

Serves 4

1kg (2¼lb) sea bass
a handful of fine salt
a good handful of fragrant herbs, cut into small pieces (e.g. rosemary, sage, thyme, marjoram)
100ml (3½fl oz) extra virgin olive oil

Wash and dry the sea bass and rub it inside and out with the salt and herbs. Arrange in an ovenproof dish, sprinkle with the oil and place in a very hot oven. Bake for 15 minutes, then cover tightly with foil. Remove the foil after 10 minutes and continue baking for another 2–3 minutes. Cut into portions while still hot and serve at once.

Delicious with artichokes with garlic and parsley.

A special meal: *branzino al forno*

Wilful Behaviour, pp. 145–146

Lunch, indeed, was something special. Perhaps it was talk of three hundred and sixty million lire that had driven Paola to excess, for she had bought an entire sea bass and baked it with fresh artichokes, lemon juice and rosemary. With it she served a platter the size of an inner tube filled with tiny roast potatoes, also lightly sprinkled with rosemary. Then, to clear the palate, a salad of rucola and radicchio. They finished with baked apples.*

'It's a good thing you have to go to the university three mornings a week and can't do this to us every day,' Brunetti said as he declined a second helping of apples.

'Am I meant to take that as a compliment?' Paola asked.

Before Brunetti could answer, Chiara asked for another apple with sufficient enthusiasm to confirm that her father's remark had indeed been a compliment.

The children astonished their parents by offering to do the dishes. Paola went back to her study and Brunetti, taking with him a glass of grappa, followed her shortly after. 'We really ought to get a new sofa, don't you think?' he said, kicking off his shoes and stretching out on the endangered piece of furniture.

'If I thought I'd ever find anything as comfortable as that one,' Paola said, 'I suppose I'd buy it.' She studied the sofa and her supine husband for some time and then said, 'Perhaps I could just have it re-covered.'

'Umm,' Brunetti agreed, eyes closed, hands clasped around the stem of his glass.

STUFFED SQUID WITH TOMATO SAUCE
Calamari ripieni al sugo di pomodoro

Serves 4

approx. 700g (1½lb) squid (4 large squid, 20cm/8 inches long)
200g (7oz) prawns, shell on
100g (3½oz) leeks
100g (3½oz) carrots
100g (3½oz) courgettes
1 medium egg
2 tablespoons breadcrumbs
a pinch of salt
freshly ground black pepper
5 tablespoons extra virgin olive oil

For the sauce

700g (1½lb) ripe tomatoes, peeled and chopped
a pinch of salt
5 tablespoons extra virgin olive oil
2 garlic cloves, finely chopped
50ml (2fl oz) fortified sweet white wine

Clean the squid, cutting off and reserving the tentacles. Peel and wash thoroughly. Shell the prawns, remove the dark thread down the back, and wash. Mince the squid tentacles and set aside. Cut the vegetables lengthways and then into slices. Place them in a non-stick pan or casserole with the oil and a pinch of salt, adding a few tablespoons of water. Cover and cook for 10 minutes, stirring frequently. Place them in a bowl and purée with a hand blender. When cool, add the egg, breadcrumbs, pepper, minced tentacles and prawns. Mix well and add salt if necessary. Fill the belly of the squid with this mixture, closing them up with toothpicks or skewers. To make the sauce, cook the tomatoes, salt, oil and garlic in a non-stick pan. When these have formed a nice smooth, thick sauce, add the wine, stir, and add the squid. Cover and cook for 20 minutes over medium heat, stirring and turning from time to time and adding a few tablespoons of water if necessary. When the squid are cooked, arrange them on a plate. Slice them finely, while keeping their shape intact, and surround with the sauce. They're delicious, and a treat for the eye as well as the palate.

Talking about school while eating *calamari ripieni*

The Girl of His Dreams, pp. 56–57

'There are *calamari ripieni* after,' Paola declared, no doubt hoping to make it easier for them to decide who wanted to finish the pasta. Chiara, who had the day before added fish and seafood to the list of things she, as a vegetarian, would not eat, opted for more pasta, as did Raffi, who would no doubt go on to pack away his sister's portion of calamari with undiminished appetite and a clear conscience. Brunetti poured himself a glass of wine and assumed the expression of a man who would never think of taking the food from the mouths of his own hungry children.

Chiara helped carry the plates back to the kitchen and returned with a dish of vegetables, while Paola brought out a platter of calamari, and he thought he could smell the carrots and leeks – perhaps even chopped shrimp – with which they were filled. Conversation was general: school, school, and school, leaving Brunetti to say he had seen the Contessa that morning and brought her love to all of them. Paola turned her head and gave him a long look when he said this, though the children found it in no way strange.

Seeing Chiara reach for the platter, Paola distracted Raffi by asking him if he and Sara Paganuzzi were still planning to go to the cinema that evening and, if so, would he like to eat something before they went? He explained that the film had been supplanted by a Greek translation Sara had still to finish, and so he would be going to her home that evening, both for dinner and to help her with the translation.

Paola asked him what the text was, and that led to a discussion of the rashness and folly of the Peloponnesian War, which both found sufficiently interesting to distract them from the sight of Brunetti and

Chiara finishing the calamari. Nor did they notice Brunetti lift his empty plate and use it to cover his daughter's.

Athens defeated and the walls destroyed, Raffi finished the vegetables and asked about dessert.

But by then the sun had disappeared, not only from Brunetti's back but from the sky, which was suddenly covered by clouds slipping in from the east. Paola got to her feet and gathered up the plates, saying there was only fruit for dessert, and they could eat it inside. Relieved, Brunetti pushed back his chair, picked up the empty vegetable bowl and the bottle of wine, and went back towards the kitchen.

Long exposure to the vagaries of springtime had chilled him sufficiently to render the thought of fruit unattractive.

STEWED BLACK CUTTLEFISH
Seppie nere in umido

Serves 4
1kg (2¼lb) cuttlefish, 10–12cm/4–5 inches long
800g (1¾lb) tinned tomatoes
100g (3½oz) white onions, thinly sliced
1 fresh chilli
1 teaspoon salt
a handful finely chopped fresh parsley
50ml (2fl oz) extra virgin olive oil
50ml (2fl oz) dry white wine

Extract the bone from the cuttlefish. From the bottom of the sac on the exterior side, remove the insides, where you will find a small pearly sac containing the ink. Set aside. Remove and discard the eyes and mouth from the centre of the tentacles. Peel and wash the cuttlefish gently. Place on a chopping board and slice crossways, removing and dividing the tentacles. Heat the oil in a large non-stick pan or casserole and cook the onion with the salt, chilli, and 100ml (3½fl oz) of water. When the onion is cooked, add the peeled tomatoes, cook until the sauce has thickened and add the cuttlefish with the small sacs of ink. Cook for a few minutes and add the parsley. Continue cooking for 20 minutes, more if necessary, so that the cuttlefish are tender. Stir often and add the white wine, a bit at a time.

Serve with hot polenta – an almost mandatory accompaniment!

Prawns with Vegetables and Coriander
Gamberoni con verdure e coriandolo

Serves 4

600g (1lb 5oz) prawns
350g (12oz) rice
300g (11oz) courgettes
300g (11oz) carrots
300g (11oz) green asparagus
50ml (2fl oz) extra virgin olive oil
300g (11oz) spring onions
salt
50g (2oz) fresh ginger, grated
a handful of fresh coriander, roughly chopped
1 garlic clove, finely chopped
1 tablespoon honey

Shell the prawns, removing the dark thread along the back. Wash, dry with kitchen paper and set aside, covered. Cut the courgettes and carrots lengthways, then into fine slices. Cut the asparagus into 2–3cm (1 inch) lengths, discarding the tough part. Boil the rice and place in an ovenproof dish and keep warm in a very low oven. Heat the oil in a large non-stick pan or casserole and add the finely sliced spring onions, a pinch of salt, a little water and half the coriander and cook for several minutes. Add the courgettes, carrots and asparagus along with the garlic and the remaining coriander. Cook over high heat for about 20 minutes, stirring often and adding a little more water if necessary. Next add the honey and ginger. Add the prawns to the pan with a pinch of salt. Stir and cook for 2 minutes, then stir everything together. Finally, arrange the prawns and vegetables on top of the rice and serve.

Eating shrimp while drinking pinot noir

The Girl of His Dreams, pp. 148–149

Because they were in a hurry, they decided not to have pasta and settled for a single dish of shrimp with vegetables and coriander. They shared a bottle of Gottardi pinot noir, turned down dessert, and finished with coffee. Feeling full but still faintly unsatisfied, Brunetti and Vianello walked out to the Accademia. Crossing the bridge, they discussed things other than what they might expect at the address they were heading towards. By unspoken agreement, they ignored the rows of *vu cumprà* who lined the steps of the bridge on both sides, confining their discussion to the sorry state of the surface of the steps and the growing need for repair or replacement of many of them.

'You think they deliberately choose materials that will wear out quickly?' Vianello asked, pointing down at one of the gaps in the surface beneath them.

'Humidity and millions of feet are just as sure to do the job for them, I think,' Brunetti said, knowing as he spoke that, however true, this explanation in no way excluded the other.

Talking idly, they crossed in front of the people seated at Paolin, eating the first *gelati* of springtime, turned left and wove their way back towards the canal.

PRAWNS IN EGG AND LIME SAUCE
Gamberoni in salsa d'uovo e lime

Serves 4

500g (1lb 2oz) prawns
4 eggs
salt and freshly ground black papper
60g (2½oz) Parmesan cheese, grated
juice of 2 limes
a pinch of oregano
50g (2oz) butter
1 garlic clove, finely chopped
50ml (2fl oz) dry white wine
1 lime

Shell the prawns, removing the dark thread along the back. Wash, dry well with kitchen paper and set aside, covered. In a bowl, beat the eggs with a pinch of salt and pepper. Add the Parmesan, then the lime juice and oregano. Heat the butter in a non-stick pan with the garlic and a pinch of salt. Add the prawns and fry briskly for 2–3 minutes, sprinkling them with the wine. Remove them and place on a plate. Add the egg mixture to the juices remaining in the pan and once thickened, pour over the prawns. Serve hot, surrounded by slices of lime.

Volatile

Though a cookbook of Venetian food is a strange place to mention this, I must confess that my mother was Irish. Well, half-Irish and half-German, but since it was her mother who was Irish, the culinary heritage which passed down through the female line was – alas – Irish. She cooked, and my brother and I, like all children everywhere, assumed that what we were given was what people were meant to eat.

More than half a century later, when I think back to some of the things we were fed, my impulse is to cover my eyes, though it might be wiser to cover my mouth. I remember meat: ham, pork, steak, lamb, chicken. There was also bacon, sausage, and hamburger: meat in all its varieties, meat in all its glory. There was also fruit: I think I owe my survival – and my brother's – to its abundance: cherries, apples, peaches, plums, oranges, bananas, and strawberries.

Many of the people I've met in the world of food insist that most cooks are either food cooks or cake cooks. If this is true, then my mother was definitely a cake cook: to her, dinner was what one ate on the way to dessert, and who can find fault in this? Give that woman a cup of sugar, a pound of butter, a dozen eggs, and a bag of flour and she became to cake what Stradivarius was to the violin. Cakes and cookies, brownies and puddings, pies and muffins flew out of her kitchen on angel wings. Christmas threw her into an orgy of cookie-making, though any day of the year was cause for Key Lime pie or fudge.

She ate like a trooper and remained rail-thin all her life, no doubt because she smoked like a Turk. There should be a monument to her in Cuba, or wherever sugar is grown today, and she would have made fast work of the European Butter Mountain. Why my brother and I were not child diabetics is one of the great mysteries of medical science.

Ah, but let me return my thoughts to the food, the real food. A few classic recipes in her repertory were spaghetti and meatballs (canned tomatoes, no garlic), fried ham steaks, and baked beans. The beans, I recall, started life in the can, which reminds me that it was not until I was living in Italy that I discovered that mayonnaise does not live in a tube but can be made from egg yolk and olive oil. But my mother's supreme culinary triumph, which has remained in the memory of all who knew her, was the Christmas turkey.

American turkeys resemble Americans in that they are significantly larger than turkeys found in other parts of the world – and those chosen to feed a family of four can be as large as ten kilos. Further, they had and still have an inordinate amount of breast, having been bred to answer the American preference for white meat. There are stories – one reads them in all the anti-globalization magazines – about the chickens who fall forward on to their beaks from the weight of their over-bred breasts. So too these poor turkeys.

Because of their size, they demanded a large oven and an enormous roasting pan, and had to be cooked for a very long time. And thus the Christmas culinary ritual as it evolved in our family.

My mother had either acquired or inherited the notion that turkey had to be well done. Now, 'well done' is a concept open to interpretation and variation, is it not? Does 'well-done' mean that blood can no longer be seen when the turkey is carved? Does it mean that the skin on the breast is crisp and dark brown? Or does it mean something more sinister?

There is a legend in the family that one of the ancestors of my mother's father was at least part American Indian, and it is only to this that I am able to attribute my mother's interest in pemmican, that dried meat which the American Indians are said to have carried with them on long journeys. Thin strips of – I believe – buffalo were suspended over open fires and slowly smoked until they were free of all moisture and thus could endure without spoiling for months, perhaps years.

No, my mother did not wear a feather head-dress while cooking the Christmas turkey, but she was clearly bent on turning it into pemmican. We had a gas oven as opposed to an open fire, but that did not deter her for an instant in her efforts: the bird was to be reduced to dried meat.

This meant that those of us who were aware of the atavistic urge of her ancestry would, during the endless hours in which the beast was being reduced to powder in the oven, see to it that my mother's glass of Christmas punch was kept full and that she was kept busy in conversation in the living room. Each time she said something about going out to the kitchen to 'check on the turkey', one of us would jump up and say, 'Oh, I was just going out to get a carrot, so I'll have a look,' or, 'Maybe I'll go stir the onions and see how it's doing.' Whoever went out to the kitchen would turn down the oven, set by my mother to a temperature just below that required to forge steel; the bolder ones turned it off. Soon the urge to check on the turkey would sweep over her, to be kept at bay only by refilling her punch glass or offering her a cigarette. A friend once introduced the brilliant variation of, 'Oh, just sit there and have another sip of punch: nothing's going to happen to that poor turkey if you do', which instantly became a Christmas standard.

Sooner or later, of course, she would make it to the kitchen and discover the lower temperature or the cooling oven. But by then she had had sufficient punch, so was inclined to blame it on her own forgetfulness, an opinion in which we all, quite mercilessly, joined her.

Finally, however, she would determine – by signs visible only to her and perhaps to American Indian ancestors – that the turkey was cooked and it was time to eat, and so we gathered around the table for the regular Christmas dinner: turkey/pemmican, onion and apple dressing, creamed parsnips, cranberry sauce, peas, and mashed potatoes (the secret of this recipe is to add *equal amounts* of potato and butter. This cannot fail).

Invariably, after grace (certainly the most embarrassing moment of the year for all of us, regardless of age or religious affiliation) we waited as my father carved the turkey, considerably reduced in size as a result of its long stay in the oven. And then we ate as much of it as we could. The napkins were the linen ones inherited from my Irish grandmother, so no one dared hide the turkey there, though my Aunt Jean, of happy memory, would eat Christmas dinner with her purse on her lap, opening it repeatedly. My Uncle Joe always brought his hunting dog to Christmas dinner, and it sat by his side for the entire meal.

Though great inroads were made on the turkey at the meal, large portions of it always remained, only to be transformed, during the week that followed, into turkey in gravy, turkey hash, and turkey sandwiches. Its disappearance was usually linked to that of the Christmas tree, though sometimes, in the form of soup, it survived even the tree.

Another cooking secret I can now reveal – my lips having been sealed by a vow of silence during her lifetime – is my mother's secret for cooking vegetables, and again this is the fruit of her Irish heritage. This recipe serves across the board and can be used for any and all vegetables, and it is with great pride that I pass it on to new cooks:

1. Open the can.
2. Pour into saucepan.
3. Add 100 grams of butter.
4. Boil until contents are reduced to a grey mush, stirring when necessary.
5. Add salt.
6. Serve.

Meat · *Carni*

Little by little, the butchers' shops of Venice are disappearing in order to make room for shops that sell glass, scarves, necklaces, masks, and shoddy goods of all sorts.

The Venetians have always been meat-eaters. In times past they ate the whole animal, and were thus able to satisfy both their taste and their pockets. There were many traditional dishes; one that has never disappeared is *La castradina*. This is a soup that is eaten on the feast day of La Madonna della Salute (21 November). It is made with smoked, spicy, sun-dried leg of mutton and sliced green Savoy cabbage. Other dishes worthy of note are *Risotto alla sbiraglia*, made with the cleaned insides, legs, cockscomb and stomach of a chicken; *La fongadina*, veal lungs cut into small pieces and cooked in a spicy sauce;

and *Il sanguetto*, made with black pudding, sliced finely and flavoured with onion.

These days, young people tend to eat only a few types of meat: roasts, chops, beefsteak, stews, boiled meats, chicken, rabbit, turkey and duck.

Yet with beef, veal, pork and lamb, hundreds of special and unusual dishes can be prepared, featuring the full palette of aromatic herbs, spices and vegetables.

So let's really appreciate our surviving butcher by going to visit him as often as we can!

Roberta Pianaro

MEAT
Carni

Chicken breast with artichokes   193
Petto di pollo ai carciofi

Chicken smothered with red Savoy cabbage   194
Pollo soffocato con verza rossa

Leg of lamb with potatoes   195
Cosciotto di agnello con patate

Lamb chops with tomatoes   196
Costolette di agnello al pomodoro

Veal fillets with fennel seeds, garlic, rosemary and bacon   201
Filetto di vitello con semi di finocchio, aglio, rosmarino, pancetta

Veal, prosciutto and artichoke roulades   205
Involtini di vitello, prosciutto e carciofi

Small veal and prosciutto meatballs   207
Polpettine di vitello e prosciutto

Veal stew with aubergines   208
Spezzatino di vitello con melanzane

Veal liver with polenta   210
Fegato di vitello con polenta

Veal shin   215
Stinco di vitello

Veal tongue in vegetable sauce   216
Lingua di vitello in salsa di verdure

CHICKEN BREAST WITH ARTICHOKES
Petto di pollo ai carciofi

Serves 4
5 medium globe artichokes
6 tablespoons extra virgin olive oil
1 teaspoon salt
1 garlic clove, finely chopped
freshly ground black pepper
750g (1lb 10oz) chicken
50ml (2fl oz) white wine
juice of ½ a lemon

Remove the tough leaves from the artichokes, trim the tips and peel the stems. Plunge into a bowl of water and lemon juice to prevent discoloration. Cut into fine slices, starting from the stems, and place in a non-stick pan or casserole with the oil, salt, garlic, pepper and at least 800ml (1 pint 8¾fl oz) of water. Cover and cook over moderate heat for about 15 minutes. Place the 2 chicken breasts at the bottom of the pan among the artichokes and after 2 minutes add the wine and continue cooking; be careful not to burn the artichokes. When the chicken is cooked, remove and cut into thin slices. Add them to the artichokes and let season. Drain and serve hot.

CHICKEN SMOTHERED WITH RED SAVOY CABBAGE
Pollo soffocato con verza rossa

Serves 4
50g (2oz) shallots, finely sliced
salt and freshly ground black pepper
8 tablespoons extra virgin olive oil
800g (1¾lb) red Savoy cabbage
4 chicken legs, skinned
100ml (3½fl oz) dry white wine

Place the shallots in a large non-stick pan with a pinch of salt, 5 tablespoons of the olive oil and a little water and fry gently for 3 minutes. Wash the cabbage and remove the outside leaves. Cut the cabbage in half and then into thin slices, discarding the core. Add to the shallot and let it wilt down to half its volume. In another large non-stick pan, fry the chicken legs with 3 tablespoons of oil, a pinch of salt and a grind of pepper until brown, sprinkling with the wine. When nicely golden, top with the cabbage, cover and lower the heat. The chicken will be cooked in about 40 minutes. Stir occasionally. Season with salt and pepper and serve hot.

LEG OF LAMB WITH POTATOES
Cosciotto di agnello con patate

Serves 4
1kg (2¼lb) leg of lamb
2 pinches of salt
a handful of fragrant fresh herbs (e.g. rosemary, thyme, marjoram, sage)
6–7 tablespoons extra virgin olive oil
100ml (3½fl oz) dry white wine

Potatoes
800g (1¾lb) potatoes, peeled and cut into chunks
a pinch of crushed fresh rosemary
1 teaspoon salt
a drizzle of extra virgin olive oil

Place the lamb in a large non-stick casserole and sprinkle with 2 pinches of salt, the herbs and the oil. Brown over a high heat, turning the lamb over. Add the wine and leave to evaporate. Then cover, lower the heat and continue cooking. Add hot water as needed to prevent the meat from sticking to the bottom of the casserole, and turn it from time to time. It will be ready after about an hour, since lamb is very tender and cooks quickly.

In the meantime, season the potatoes and bake in the oven at high heat for 45 minutes. Serve the meat and potatoes together, very hot.

LAMB CHOPS WITH TOMATOES
Costolette di agnello al pomodoro

Serves 4
10 tablespoons extra virgin olive oil
2 garlic cloves, finely chopped
a handful of fragrant fresh herbs (e.g. rosemary, sage, bay leaf, thyme, marjoram)
a pinch of dried chilli flakes
2 teaspoons salt
8 tomatoes, peeled and chopped
800g (1¾lb) lamb chops

Heat the oil in a large non-stick pan and lightly fry the garlic with the herbs and chilli. Then add 200ml (7fl oz) of water (more if needed), the salt and the tomatoes. When the sauce has cooked and thickened (this should take about 25 minutes), add the lamb chops and cook over moderate heat, stirring just once, for 15 minutes or more depending on thickness.

If desired, you can accompany this dish with boiled basmati rice.

For the rice
300g (11oz) basmati rice
1 teaspoon salt

Put the rice and salt into a medium-sized non-stick pan and add 500ml (18fl oz) of water. Cover and cook over moderate heat for about 20 minutes, by which time the water should be completely absorbed. Arrange in a dish with the lamb chops and sauce and serve.

What better for a Persian friend than lamb chops?

Blood from a Stone, pp. 270–275

When he entered, shoeless, he found a stranger at his table: a young girl sat in Raffi's place. She got to her feet as he came into the kitchen. Chiara said, 'This is my friend, Azir Mahani.'

'Hello,' Brunetti said and put out his hand.

The girl looked at him, at his hand, and then at Chiara, who said, 'Shake his hand, silly. He's my father.'

The girl leaned forward, but she did so stiffly, and put out her hand as if suspecting Brunetti might not give it back. He took it and held it briefly, as though it were a kitten, a particularly fragile one. He was curious about her shyness but said nothing more than hello and that he was glad she could join them for lunch.

He waited for the girl to seat herself, but she seemed to be waiting for him. Chiara reached up and yanked at the bottom of the girl's sweater, saying, 'Oh, sit down, Azir. He's going to eat his lunch, not you.' The girl blushed and sat down. She looked at her plate.

Seeing this, Chiara got up and went over to Brunetti. 'Azir, look,' she said. As soon as she had her friend's attention, Chiara bent down and stared directly into Brunetti's eyes, saying, 'I am going to hypnotize you with the power of my gaze and put you into a deep sleep.'

Instantly, Brunetti closed his eyes.

'Are you asleep?' Chiara asked.

'Yes,' Brunetti said in a sleepy voice, letting his head fall forward on his chest. Paola, who had had no time to greet Brunetti, turned back to the stove and continued filling four dishes with pasta.

Before she spoke again, Chiara made a business of waving her open hand back and forth in front of Brunetti's eyes, to show Azir that he was really asleep. She leaned down and spoke into his left ear, dragging out the final syllable in every word. 'Who is the most wonderful daughter in the whole world?'

Brunetti, keeping his eyes closed, mumbled something.

Chiara gave him an irritated glance, bent even closer and asked, 'Who is the most wonderful daughter in the whole world?'

Brunetti fluttered his eyelids, indicating that the question had finally registered. In a voice he made intentionally indistinct, he began, speaking as slowly as had Chiara, 'The most wonderful daughter in the world is . . .'

Chiara, triumph at hand, stepped back to hear the magic name.

Brunetti raised his head, opened his eyes, and said, 'Is Azir,' but as a consolation prize, he grabbed Chiara and pulled her close, kissing her on the ear. Paola chose this moment to turn from the stove and say, 'Chiara, would you be a wonderful daughter and help serve?'

As Chiara set a dish of pappardelle with porcini* in front of Brunetti, he sneaked a glance across the table at Azir, relieved to see she had survived the ordeal of being mentioned by name.

Chiara took her place and picked up her fork. Suddenly she looked suspiciously at her pasta and said, 'There isn't any ham in this, is there, Mamma?'

Surprised, Paola said, 'Of course not. Never, with porcini.' Then, 'Why do you ask?'

'Because Azir can't eat it.' Hearing this, Brunetti consciously kept his eyes on his own daughter and did not glance at the most wonderful one in the whole world.

'Of course she can't, Chiara. I know that.' Then, to Azir, 'I hope you like lamb, Azir. I thought we'd have broiled lamb chops.'

'Yes, Signora,' Azir said, the first words she had spoken since what Brunetti had come to think of as her ordeal began. There was a trace of an accent, but only a trace.

'I was going to try to make *fessenjoon*,' Paola said, 'but then I thought your mother probably makes it much better than I could, so I decided to stick with the chops.'

'You know about *fessenjoon*?' Azir asked, her face brightening.

Paola smiled around a mouthful of pappardelle. 'Well, I've made it once or twice, but it's hard to find the right spices here, and especially the pomegranate juice.'

'Oh, my mother has some bottles my aunt brought her. I'm sure she'd give you one,' Azir said, and as her face took on animation, Brunetti saw how lovely she was: sharp nose, almond eyes, and two wings of the blackest hair he had ever seen swinging down alongside her jaw.

'Oh, that would be lovely. Then maybe you could come and help me cook it,' Paola said.

'I'd like that,' Azir said. 'I'll ask my mother to write it down, the recipe.'

'I can't read Farsi, I'm afraid,' Paola said in what sounded very much like an apologetic tone.

'Would English be all right?' Azir asked.

'Of course,' Paola said, then looked around the table. 'Would anyone like more pasta?'

When no one volunteered, she started to reach for the plates, but Azir got to her feet and cleared the table without being asked. She attached herself to Paola at the counter and happily carried the platter of lamb to the table, then a large bowl of rice and after that a platter of grilled radicchio.*

'How is it that your mother speaks English?' Paola asked.

'She taught it at the university in Esfahan,' Azir said. 'Until we left.'

Though the word hung in the air, no one asked Azir why her family had decided to leave or if, in fact, it had been their decision.

The girl had eaten very little of her pasta, but she dug into the lamb and rice with a vigour that even Chiara found hard to match. Brunetti watched the tiny curved bones pile up on the sides of the plates of the two girls, marvelled at the mounds of rice that seemingly evaporated as soon as they got within a centimetre of their forks.

After a time, Paola took both the platter and the bowl back to the sink and refilled them, leaving Brunetti impressed at how she had foreseen this adolescent plague of locusts. Azir, after saying that she had never eaten radicchio and had no idea what it was, allowed Paola to pile some on her plate. While no one was watching, it disappeared.

When offers of more food met with honest protests, Paola and Azir cleared the table, and Paola handed the girl smaller plates and fruit dishes. Then she opened the refrigerator and pulled out a large bowl of chopped fruit.

Paola asked who wanted *macedonia*, and Azir asked, 'Why is it called that, Dottoressa?'

'I think because of the country, Macedonia, which is made up of small groups of people who have been all cut up and segmented. But I'm not sure.' She turned to Chiara and, as was usual in such situations, said, 'Get the Zanichelli, Chiara.'

Because the dictionary was now kept in Chiara's room, she disappeared and returned with the heavy volume. She opened the book and started flipping pages, muttering under her breath as she went: '*macchia*', '*macchiare*', '*macedone*', until she finally found the right place and read out, 'Macedonia', and the origin, proving Paola's guess correct. After that her voice dropped into the mumble of a person reading to herself. She slid her plate to one side and replaced it with the open book. Then, as if the other people at the table had evaporated along with the rice, she began to read the other entries on the page.

Azir finished her fruit, refused a second helping, and got to her feet saying, 'May I help you with the dishes, Signora?'

Brunetti pushed back his chair and went into the living room, thinking that perhaps he had been mistaken about Chiara all these years and Azir really was the most wonderful daughter in the whole world.

Veal Fillets with Fennel Seeds, Garlic, Rosemary and Bacon

Filetto di vitello con semi di finocchio, aglio, rosmarino, pancetta

Serves 4

8 thin slices of smoked bacon
4 slices of veal fillet, each about 160g (5½oz)
salt and freshly ground black pepper
2 pinches of fennel seeds
30g (1oz) butter
3 tablespoons extra virgin olive oil
1 garlic clove, halved and slightly crushed
2 sprigs of fresh rosemary

Roll the bacon round the veal slices, tying with kitchen string. Sprinkle the rolls with salt and pepper and press the fennel seeds into the surface. Heat the butter, oil, garlic and rosemary and stir briskly in a non-stick pan large enough to hold everything side by side. Place the veal rolls in the pan, side by side, then lower the heat and cook for 5–6 minutes, turning once. Serve immediately.

Are we allowed to make mad zucchini jokes?
Eating *filetto di vitello*

Uniform Justice, pp. 174–177

Because Raffi as well as Chiara was at dinner, and because he thought it unseemly to manifest pride in such mean-spirited behaviour in their presence, he said nothing about his meeting with the cadets and contented himself with the meal. Paola had brought home *ravioli di zucca** and had prepared them with salvia leaves quickly sautéed in butter, then smothered them with Parmigiano. After that, she had switched to fennel, serving it interspersed with pan-fried veal pieces that had been cooked with rosemary, garlic, fennel seed and wrapped in pancetta.

As he ate, delighted by the mingled tastes and the pleasant sharpness of his third glass of Sangiovese, he remembered his earlier uneasiness about the safety of his children, and the thought made him feel foolish. He could not, however, dismiss it or allow himself to scoff at the desire that nothing would ever invade their peace. He never knew if his perpetual readiness for things to change for the worse was the result of his native pessimism or of the experiences his profession had exposed him to. In either case, his vision of happiness had always to pass through a filter of uneasiness.

'Why don't we ever have beef any more?' Raffi asked.

Paola, peeling a pear, said, 'Because Gianni can't find a farmer he trusts.'

'Trusts to do what?' Chiara asked between grapes.

'To have animals he's sure are healthy, I suppose,' Paola answered.

'I don't like eating it any more, anyway,' Chiara said.

'Why not? Because it'll make you crazy?' her brother asked, then amended it to 'Crazier?'

'I think we've had more than enough mad-cow jokes at this table,' Paola said with an unusual lack of patience.

'No, not because of that,' Chiara said.

'Then why?' Brunetti asked.

'Oh, just because,' Chiara answered evasively.

'Because of what?' her brother asked.

'Because we don't need to eat them.'

'That never bothered you before,' Raffi countered.

'I know it never bothered me before. Lots of things didn't. But now they do.' She turned to him and delivered what she clearly thought would be a death blow. 'It's called growing up, in case you've never heard of it.'

Raffi snorted, driving her to new defences.

'We don't need to eat them just because we can. Besides, it's ecologically wasteful,' she insisted, like someone repeating a lesson, which Brunetti thought was most likely the case.

'What would you eat instead?' Raffi asked, 'Zucchini?' He turned to his mother and asked, 'Are we allowed to make mad-zucchini jokes?'

Paola, displaying the Olympian disregard for the feelings of her children which Brunetti so admired, said only, 'I'll take that as an offer to do the dishes, Raffi, shall I?'

Raffi groaned, but he did not protest. A Brunetti less familiar with the cunning of the young would have seen this as a sign that his son was willing to assume some responsibility for the care of their home, perhaps as evidence of burgeoning maturity. The real Brunetti, however, a man hardened by decades of exposure to the furtiveness of criminals, could see it for what it was: cold-blooded bargaining in which immediate acquiescence was traded for some future reward.

As Raffi reached across the table to pick up his mother's plate, Paola smiled upon him with favour and, displaying a familiarity with slyness equal to that of her husband, got to her feet, saying, 'Thank you so much, dear, for offering, and no, you cannot take scuba lessons.'

Brunetti watched her leave the room, then turned to watch his son's face. Raffi's surprise was patent, and when he saw that his father was looking at him, he removed that expression but had the grace to smile. 'How does she do that?' Raffi asked. 'All the time.'

Brunetti was about to offer some bromide about its being one of the powers of mothers to be able to read the minds of their children, when Chiara, who had been busy finishing the fruit on the platter, looked up at them and said, 'It's because she reads Henry James.'

Veal, Prosciutto and Artichoke Roulades
Involtini di vitello, prosciutto e carciofi

Serves 4

4 medium globe artichokes

juice of ½ a lemon

8 slices of leg of veal, each around 100g (3½oz) (ask your butcher to cut these for you)

8 thin slices of raw prosciutto

4 tablespoons extra virgin olive oil

60g (2½oz) butter, cut into small cubes

100ml (3½fl oz) dry white wine

salt and freshly ground black pepper

Clean the artichokes, discarding the tough leaves and trimming the tips. Cut them in half, removing the choke, and plunge them into a bowl of cold water with the lemon juice. Let them soak for a little while, then drain and dry well. Place a veal slice on the chopping board, cover with a slice of prosciutto, then wrap both around an artichoke half, starting from the narrowest part. Close the roulade with toothpicks or skewers (these can be removed once the rolls have browned). No salt is needed because the prosciutto is already salty. Continue in the same way with the remaining 7 slices and arrange the rolls in the bottom of a large non-stick pan or casserole. Add the oil and the butter and brown the rolls. When golden add the wine, allow to evaporate, lower the heat, cover and continue cooking, adding hot water from time to time. The roulades should be turned often and cooked for at least 1 hour so that the artichokes will be almost creamy. Taste and add salt if necessary, sprinkle with a pinch of pepper and serve hot.

Small Veal and Prosciutto Meatballs
Polpettine di vitello e prosciutto

Serves 4
250g (9oz) ground veal
150g (5oz) oven-baked prosciutto, finely chopped
150g (5oz) ricotta cheese
a pinch of salt
1 medium egg
50g (2oz) Parmesan cheese, grated
50g (2oz) fresh root ginger, grated
flour
200ml (7fl oz) sunflower oil

Place the veal and prosciutto in a mixing bowl and add the ricotta, salt, egg and Parmesan. Mix thoroughly, using your hands, then add the ginger and mix again. Form the mixture into small balls, slightly 'squashed' and larger than a walnut. Coat lightly with flour and place on a large plate. Heat the oil in a large frying pan over a high heat, add the meatballs in one layer and fry for 3–4 minutes, turning. Drain on absorbent paper and serve hot.

VEAL STEW WITH AUBERGINES
Spezzatino di vitello con melanzane

Serves 4

For the stew

8 tablespoons extra virgin olive oil
1 sprig of fresh rosemary
1 sprig of fresh sage
a pinch of salt
800g (1¾lb) stewing veal
100ml (3½fl oz) dry white wine

For the aubergines

2–3 aubergines about 15cm (6 inches) long
10 tablespoons extra virgin olive oil
1 garlic clove, halved
a pinch of salt
freshly ground black pepper

For the stew, place the oil in a non-stick casserole over high heat and add the herbs, salt and veal. Brown the meat, then add the wine, cook until evaporated, and add 400ml (14fl oz) of hot water. Lower the heat, then cover the pan and cook for at least 1 hour and 20 minutes, turning the meat often, adding hot water and check the seasoning. Be careful not to let the meat stick to the bottom of the casserole.

In the meantime remove the stems from the aubergines and dice them. Heat the oil in a non-stick pan and fry the garlic lightly with the salt, being careful not to burn it. Add the aubergines and stir in. After a few minutes, lower the heat and continue cooking for at least 20 minutes, adding a little hot water, until the aubergines are soft. When the meat is very tender place without the cooking sauce, on top of the aubergines. Sprinkle with pepper and serve hot.

VEAL LIVER WITH POLENTA
Fegato di vitello con polenta

Serves 4

For the veal

50ml (2fl oz) extra virgin olive oil

200g (7oz) white onions, sliced

salt and freshly ground black pepper

500g (1lb 2oz) veal liver, cut into thin slices, then into squares (ask your butcher to do this for you)

For the polenta

250g (9oz) yellow polenta

salt

Put the oil, onions, a pinch of salt and 100ml (3½fl oz) of water into a non-stick pan and cook over moderate heat for 20 minutes, stirring often, until the onion is transparent but not burnt, and the water has evaporated. Set aside.

Boil 1 litre (1¾ pints) of salted water in a large non-stick pan and pour in the polenta. Stir constantly with a whisk until amalgamated, then cover and cook for 40 minutes over moderate heat, still stirring from time to time and adding hot water if needed – the polenta should be fairly soft. When cooked, place the polenta in a large serving dish with a border, leaving a circular space in the centre for the liver. Return the pan with the onions to the heat. When they start to fry, add the liver and a pinch of salt. Cook for 3 minutes, stirring, add a grind of pepper and arrange in the centre of the polenta. Serve at once.

A classic Venetian dish: liver and polenta

Death in a Strange Country, pp. 72–76

'*Ciao*, Guido,' she said, standing. 'Dinner in ten minutes.' She kissed him, turned back to the stove, where onions were browning in a pool of oil.

'I just had a literary discussion with our daughter,' he said. 'She was explaining the plot of a great classic of English literature to me. I think it might be better for her if we forced her to watch the Brazilian soap operas on television. She's in there, rooting for the fire to kill Mrs Rochester.'

'Oh, come on, Guido, everyone roots for the fire when they read *Jane Eyre*.' She stirred the onions around in the pan and added, 'Well, at least the first time they read it. It isn't until later that they realize what a cunning, self-righteous little bitch Jane Eyre really is.'

'Is that the kind of thing you tell your students?' he asked, opening a cabinet and pulling out a bottle of Pinot Noir.

The liver lay sliced and waiting on a plate beside the frying pan. Paola slipped a slotted ladle under it and flipped half into the pan, then stepped back to avoid the spitting oil. She shrugged. Classes at the university had just resumed, and she obviously didn't want to think about students on her own time.

Stirring, she asked, 'What was the captain-doctor like?'

He pulled down two glasses and poured wine into both. He leaned back against the worktop, handed her one, sipped, answered, 'Very young and very nervous.' Seeing that Paola continued to stir, he added, 'And very pretty.'

Hearing that, she sipped at the glass she held in one hand and looked at him.

'Nervous about what?' She took another sip of the wine, held the glass up to the light, and said, 'This isn't as good as what we got from Mario, is it?'

'No,' he agreed. 'But your cousin Mario is so busy making a name for himself in the international wine trade that he doesn't have time to bother with orders as small as ours.'

'He would if we paid him on time,' she snapped.

'Paola, come on. That was six months ago.'

'And it was more than six months that we kept him waiting to be paid.'

'Paola, I'm sorry. I thought I'd paid him, and then I forgot about it. I apologized to him.'

She set the glass down and gave the liver a quick jab.

'Paola, it was only two hundred thousand lire. That's not going to send your cousin Mario to the poorhouse.'

'Why do you always call him, "my cousin Mario?"'

Brunetti came within a hair's breadth of saying, 'Because he's your cousin and his name is Mario,' but, instead, set his glass down on the worktop and put his arms around her. For a long time, she remained stiff, leaning away from him. He increased the pressure of his arms around her, and she relaxed, leaned against him, and put her head back against his chest.

They stayed like that until she poked him in the ribs with the end of the spoon and said, 'Liver's burning.'

He released her and picked up his glass again.

'I don't know what she's nervous about, but it upset her to see the corpse.'

'Wouldn't anyone be upset to see a dead man, especially someone they knew?'

'No, it was more than that. I'm sure there was something between them.'

'What sort of something?'

'The usual sort.'

'Well, you said she was pretty.'

He smiled. 'Very pretty.' She smiled. 'And very,' he began,

searching for the right word. The right one didn't make any sense. 'And very frightened.'

'Why do you say that?' Paola asked, carrying the pan to the table and setting it down on a ceramic tile. 'Frightened about what? That she'd be suspected of killing him?'

From beside the stove, he took the large wooden cutting board and carried it to the table. He sat and lifted the kitchen towel spread across the board and exposed the half-wheel of golden polenta that lay, still warm and now grown firm, beneath it. She brought a salad and the bottle of wine, pouring them both more before she sat down.

'No, I don't think it's that,' he said, and spooned liver and onions onto his plate, then added a broad wedge of polenta. He speared a piece of liver with his fork, pushed onions on top of it with his knife, and began to eat. As was his habit, he said nothing until his plate was empty. When the liver was gone and he was mopping the juice up with what remained of his second helping of polenta, he said, 'I think she might know, or have some idea about, who killed him. Or why he was killed.'

'Why?'

'If you'd seen her look when she saw him. No, not when she saw that he was dead and that it was really Foster, but when she saw what killed him – she was on the edge of panic. She got sick.'

'Sick?'

'Threw up.'

'Right there?'

'Yes. Strange, isn't it?'

Paola thought for a while before she answered. She finished her wine, poured herself another half-glass. 'Yes. It's a strange reaction to death. And she's a doctor?' He nodded. 'Makes no sense. What could she be afraid of?'

'Anything for dessert?'

'Figs.'

'I love you.'

'You mean you love figs,' she said and smiled.

There were six of them, perfect and moist with sweetness. He took his knife and began to peel one. When he was done, juice running down both hands, he cut it in half and handed the larger piece to her.

He crammed most of the other into his mouth and wiped at the juice that ran down his chin. He finished the fig, ate two more, wiped at his mouth again, cleaned his hands on his napkin, and said, 'If you give me a small glass of port, I'll die a happy man.'

VEAL SHIN
Stinco di vitello

Serves 5–6

1 veal shin of approx. 2.5kg (5½lb), with bone
salt
a handful of fragrant herbs (e.g. sage, rosemary, bay leaf)
100ml (3½fl oz) extra virgin olive oil
200ml (7fl oz) dry white wine

Season the veal with salt. Place in a roasting pan, cover with the herbs, pour over the oil and put in an oven preheated to the maximum temperature. Brown for 1 hour, turning the meat and dousing with the wine from time to time. When browned, cover with foil and continue cooking, adding hot water frequently so the bottom of the veal doesn't burn. After 2 hours the meat will be tender. At the end of cooking, drain off the pan juices, strain into a sauce boat and keep warm. Place the veal on a large serving platter. Carve it just before serving and sprinkle each slice with the pan juices.

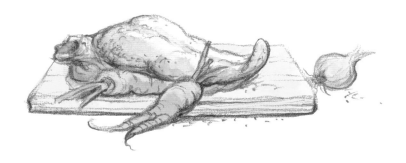

Veal Tongue in Vegetable Sauce
Lingua di vitello in salsa di verdure

Serves 4
1 celery stalk
1 small carrot
1 small onion
1 veal tongue
salt

For the sauce
100g (3½oz) celery, finely chopped
100g (3½oz) carrot, finely chopped
60g (2½oz) shallots, finely chopped
6 tablespoons extra virgin olive oil
salt and freshly ground black pepper
1 sprig of fresh parsley, finely chopped
1 garlic clove, finely chopped
50g (2oz) capers in vinegar, finely chopped
2 tablespoons white wine vinegar

Put the celery stalk, carrot and onion into a large pan of boiling salted water. Add the tongue, reduce the heat and cook for 1½ hours. To make the sauce, place the finely chopped celery, carrot and shallots in a pan or casserole with 3 tablespoons of oil, a pinch of salt and 600ml (1 pint) of water. Cover and cook over moderate heat for at least 40 minutes, adding water from time to time. Remove the casserole from the heat and add the parsley, garlic and capers. Check the seasoning for salt and add the remaining 3 tablespoons of oil, then add the vinegar and a good grind of pepper. Return to the heat for another 2 minutes. The sauce should not be watery. Remove the tongue from its broth and drain. Peel, slice finely, arrange on a plate and cover with the sauce. Serve lukewarm.

Beef, Pepper, Onion and Carrot Stew
Ragù di manzo con peperoni, cipolla, carote

Serves 4

For the meat
3 tablespoons extra virgin olive oil
50g (2oz) shallots, finely chopped
a pinch of salt
1 bay leaf
1 fresh chilli, cut into small pieces
220g (8oz) minced beef
300g (11oz) tomato purée

For the sauce
3 tablespoons extra virgin olive oil
100g (3½oz) white onion, thinly sliced
200g (7oz) carrots, thinly sliced
a pinch of salt
400g (14oz) yellow peppers, deseeded and thinly sliced

Heat the oil in a casserole and cook the shallots with the salt, bay leaf, chilli and a little water for 2 minutes. Add the minced beef and cook, stirring, until browned. Add the tomato purée, lower the heat, cover, and cook for at least 1 hour and 20 minutes. Add a little hot water from time to time, stirring, and adjust the seasoning.

Meanwhile, make the sauce. Heat the oil in a non-stick pan and fry the onions and carrots with the salt for a few minutes. Add the peppers and cook for another 20 minutes, stirring often. When the meat sauce has reduced, add it to the vegetables.

This is a superb sauce for pasta.

Vegetarian alert! beef stew

A Sea of Troubles, pp. 236–238

Chiara started to speak, but Raffi gave her a sharp kick under the table, and her head swung towards him. He pressed his lips together and narrowed his eyes at her, and she stopped.

Silence fell, then lay, on the table. 'Yes,' Brunetti said, clearing his throat and then continuing. 'I went out to Burano to talk to someone, but he wasn't there. I tried to eat at da Romano, but there were no tables.' He finished his lasagne and looked across at Paola. 'Is there any more? It's delicious,' he added.

'What else is there, *Mamma*?' Chiara demanded, appetite overcoming Raffi's warning.

'Beef stew with peppers,' Paola asked.

'The one with potatoes?' Raffi asked, his voice rich with feigned enthusiasm.

'Yes,' Paola said, getting to her feet and starting to stack the plates. The lasagne, to Brunetti's disappointment, proved to be much like the Messiah: there was no second coming.

With Paola busy at the stove, Chiara waved a hand to get Brunetti's attention, then tilted her head to one side, gaped her mouth open and stuck out her tongue. She crossed her eyes and tilted her head to the other side, then turned it into a metronome, shaking it quickly back and forth, her tongue lolling slackly from her mouth.

From her place at the stove, where she was busy serving the stew, Paola said, 'If you think this beef will give you Mad Cow Disease, Chiara, perhaps you'd prefer not to eat any.'

Instantly, Chiara's head was motionless, her hands folded neatly in front of her. 'Oh, no, *Mamma*,' she said with oily piety, 'I'm very hungry, and you know it's one of my favourites.'

'Everything's your favourite,' Raffi said.

She stuck her tongue out again, but this time her head remained motionless.

Paola turned back to the table, placing a dish in front of Chiara, then Raffi. She set another in front of Brunetti and then served herself. She sat down.

'What did the children do at school today?' Brunetti asked the children jointly, hoping that one of them would answer. As he ate, his attention drifted from the chunks of stewed beef to the cubes of carrot, the small slices of onion. Raffi was saying something about his Greek instructor. When he paused, Brunetti looked across at Paola and asked, 'Did you put Barbera in this?'

She nodded, and he smiled, pleased he'd got it right.

PORK STEW WITH PORCINI AND POLENTA
Ragù di maiale con funghi porcini e polenta

Serves 4

For the meat sauce
100g (3½oz) onions, finely chopped
a pinch of fragrant herbs, finely chopped (e.g. rosemary, sage, thyme)
a pinch of salt
10 tablespoons extra virgin olive oil
400g (14oz) lean minced pork
600g (1lb 5oz) tomato purée
2 teaspoons crushed meat stock cube
freshly ground black pepper

For the mushrooms
600g (1lb 5oz) porcini mushrooms, or 600g (1lb 5oz) white mushrooms,
    stems removed
4 tablespoons extra virgin olive oil
1 garlic clove, halved
a pinch of salt
a pinch of finely chopped fresh parsley

For the polenta
250g (9oz) yellow polenta
salt

Place the onions, herbs, salt, oil and 2 tablespoons of water in a non-stick casserole and cook for 2 minutes, being careful not to burn the onion. Add the meat, stir and cook until browned. Add the tomato purée and the crushed stock cube with a little hot water. Lower the heat, cover and cook for at least 2 hours. Stir frequently, adding hot water as necessary. Season with salt and pepper.

Wash the mushrooms and slice finely. Heat the oil in a non-stick pan with high sides and sizzle the garlic with the salt, being careful not to burn it. Add the mushrooms and cook over a high heat, stirring often and adding the parsley halfway through. The mushrooms will be ready when only the oil can be seen at the bottom of the casserole. Remove from the heat, discard the garlic and keep hot. Pour 1 litre (1¾ pints) of water into a large non-stick pan and add the salt. Bring to the boil, and pour in the polenta, stirring with a whisk. When well mixed and lump-free, cover the pan and cook for at least 40 minutes, stirring from time to time and adding more water as necessary – the polenta should be soft. Season, then arrange in a large serving dish with the hot meat sauce in the middle and the mushrooms on top. Serve at once.

For those times when the porcini are fresh: pork with porcini

The Death of Faith, pp. 176–180

'You think the kids would like to go out to dinner?' he asked.

'No, they're watching some stupid movie that won't be over until eight, and I've already got something cooking.'

'What?' he asked, realizing that he was very hungry.

'Gianni had some beautiful pork today.'

'Good. How are you cooking it?'

'With porcini.'

'And polenta?'

She smiled at him. 'Of course. No wonder you're getting that stomach.'

'What stomach?' Brunetti asked, pulling in the one he had. When she didn't answer, Brunetti said, 'It's the end of the winter.' To divert her, perhaps to divert himself from discussion of his stomach, he explained the events of the day (…)

'You mean somebody is trying to kill her?'

He nodded.

'Why?'

'That would depend on whom she's been to see since she spoke to me. And what she told them.'

'Would she be that rash?' Paola asked. The only things she knew about Maria Testa had come from what Brunetti had said about Suor'Immacolata over the years, and they had always been in praise of her patience and charity as a nun, hardly the sort of information that would give her any idea of how the young woman might behave in a situation such as the one Brunetti had described.

'I don't think she'd even think it was rash. She's been a nun most of her life, Paola,' he said as though that would explain everything.

'What is that supposed to mean?'

'That she doesn't have a very clear idea of how people behave. She probably hasn't been exposed to human evil or to deceit.'

'You said she was Sicilian, didn't you?' Paola asked.

'That's not funny.'

'I didn't mean it as a joke, Guido,' Paola said, voice injured. 'I'm quite serious. If she grew up in that society . . .' She turned away from the stove. 'How old did you say she was when she joined?'

'Fifteen, I think.'

'Then, if she grew up in Sicily, she had sufficient exposure to human behaviour to accept the possibility of evil. Don't romanticize her. She's not a plaster saint who will collapse at the first sight of impropriety or misbehaviour.'

Brunetti couldn't keep the resentment out of his voice when he shot back, 'Killing five old people can hardly be considered misbehaviour.' Paola made no rejoinder, merely stared at him and then turned to add salt to the boiling water.

'All right, all right, I know there's not much proof,' he temporized,

and then when Paola refused to turn around, he corrected even that. 'All right, no proof. But then why would there be a rumour that she had stolen the money and hurt one of the old people? And why would she have been hit and left by the road?'

Paola opened the package of dry corn meal that stood next to the pot and grabbed up a handful. As she spoke, she trickled a fine stream into the boiling water with one hand, stirring with the other. 'It could have been a hit and run,' she said. 'And women alone don't have much to do except gossip,' she added.

Brunetti sat with his mouth open. 'And this,' he finally said, 'this from a woman who considers herself a feminist? Heaven save me from hearing what women who are not feminists say about women who live alone.'

'I mean it, Guido. Women or men, it's all the same.' Undisturbed by his opposition, she continued to dribble the corn meal into the boiling water, slowly stirring all the while. 'Leave people alone long enough, and all they can do is gossip about one another. It's worse if there are no diversions.'

'Like sex?' he asked, hoping to shock her or at least to make her laugh.

'Especially if there is no sex.'

She finished adding the corn meal, and Brunetti considered what they had both just said.

'Here, stir this while I set the table,' she said, standing aside and leaving the place in front of the stove free. She held the wooden spoon out to him.

'I'll set the table,' he said, getting up and opening the cabinet. Slowly, he laid out the plates, glasses, and silverware. 'We having salad?' he asked. When Paola nodded, he pulled down four salad plates and placed them on the counter. 'Dessert?' he asked.

'Fruit.'

He pulled down four more plates.

He sat back in his place and picked up his glass. He took a sip, swallowed, and said, 'All right. Maybe it was an accident, and maybe it's entirely accidental that they're speaking badly of her in the *casa di cura.*' He set the glass down and poured some more wine into it. 'Is that what you think?'

She gave the polenta another stir and placed the wooden spoon across the open top. 'No, I think someone tried to kill her. And I think someone planted the story about taking the money. Everything you've ever said about her tells me it's impossible that she would lie or steal. And I doubt that anyone who knew her well would believe it. Not unless the story came from someone in a position of authority.' She picked up his glass and took a sip, then set the glass down.

CHINE OF PORK WITH MUSHROOMS
Arista di maiale con funghi

Serves 4
900g (2lb) pork chine, sliced
salt
a handful of fragrant herbs (e.g. rosemary, thyme, sage)
100ml (3½fl oz) dry white wine
50ml (2fl oz) extra virgin olive oil

For the mushrooms
300g (11oz) button mushrooms, caps only
1 tablespoon extra virgin olive oil
30g (1oz) butter
1 garlic clove, finely chopped
a pinch of salt
freshly ground black pepper

Place the pork slices in a casserole with the oil. Sprinkle with the salt and crushed herbs and brown over a high heat. Add the wine, allow to evaporate, then cover and lower the heat. Continue to cook for 1½ hours, adding 1 litre (1¾ pints) of hot water, a little at a time, checking that the meat doesn't stick to the pan.

Wash and dry the mushrooms, slice finely and place in a pan with the oil, butter, garlic and salt. Cook them for at least 15 minutes, until the mushroom liquid has cooked away completely. Remove the pork slices from the casserole to a serving dish. Strain the liquid and add it to the mushrooms with a generous grind of pepper. Pour the mushroom sauce over the pork and serve hot.

A different flavour: pork with mushrooms

The Girl of His Dreams, pp. 278–280

He broached the subject at dinner, between the risotto with spinach and the pork with mushrooms. Chiara – who appeared to have abandoned vegetarianism – looked somehow different that evening, said that she didn't know Ludovica Fornari but knew of her.

'Of?' Brunetti asked, placing another piece of pork on his plate.

'Even I've heard about her,' Raffi offered, then returned his attention to the bowl of carrots with ginger.*

'What have you heard?' Brunetti enquired mildly.

Paola shot him a glance as sharp as it was suspicious and interrupted to ask, 'Chiara, is that my Passion Flower you're wearing?' Brunetti had no idea to what the name referred. Because Chiara was wearing a white cotton sweater, it was not likely to be an article of clothing: that left lipstick or whatever else might be applied to a face. Or perfume, though he had not been aware of any, and Paola usually never wore scent.

'Yes,' Chiara said with a certain hesitation.

'I thought so,' Paola said with a wide smile. 'It looks very good on you.' She tilted her head to one side and studied her daughter's face. 'Probably better on you than it does on me, so maybe you'd better keep it.'

'You don't mind, do you, *Mamma*?' Chiara asked.

'No, no, not at all.' Looking brightly around the table, Paola said, 'There's only fruit for dessert, but I think tonight might be a good time to open the *gelato* season. Anyone willing to go over to Giacomo dell'Orio to get it?'

Raffi speared the remaining wheels of carrot and put them into his mouth, set his fork down, and raised his hand. 'I'll go.'

'But what about flavours?' Paola, who had never in her life shown any interest at all in the flavours of ice cream she ate – so long as she got a lot of it – asked with transparently false brightness. 'Chiara, why don't you go with your brother and help him decide?'

Chiara pushed her chair back and got to her feet. 'How much?'

'Get the biggest container they have: we should begin the year with a bang, I think.' Then, to Raffi, 'Take the money from my purse. It's near the door.'

Before Brunetti could finish his dinner and in open defiance of family tradition, the children were out the door and pounding down the stairs.

Brunetti set his fork down, conscious in the silence of the sound it made as it tapped the wood of the table. 'And what was that all about, if I might ask?' he said.

'It's about not turning my children into spies,' Paola said heatedly. Then, before he could begin to defend himself, she added, 'And don't say you were just asking idle questions, making conversation over dinner. I know you too well to believe that, Guido. And I won't have it.'

Brunetti looked at his plate, suddenly wondering how he had managed to eat so much, for why else would he suddenly feel so uncomfortably full? He sipped the last of his wine and set the glass back on the table.

She was right. He knew that, but it angered him to have it pointed out to him so sharply. He looked at his plate again, picked up his fork and set it across the plate, then placed the knife in a neat parallel next to it.

'And, Guido, you wouldn't have it, either, not really,' she said in a far softer voice. 'I said I knew you too well.' There was a pause, and then she said, 'You wouldn't like it if you had done it.'

He pushed his chair back and got to his feet. He picked up his plate to carry it into the kitchen. Behind her chair he stopped and put his hand on her shoulder; hers covered his immediately.

'I hope they bring some chocolate,' he said, his appetite suddenly restored.

Pork Shin with Green Olives
Stinco di maiale con olive verdi

Serves 4

3 pork shins with the bone, 500–600g (1–1½lb) each
salt
a handful of fresh sage and rosemary, crushed
50ml (2fl oz) extra virgin olive oil
200ml (7fl oz) dry white wine
200g (7oz) green olives, stoned and minced
50g (2oz) butter
freshly ground black pepper

Lay the shins out on a non-stick roasting pan and sprinkle with the salt, herbs and oil. Place in an oven preheated to 240°C/475°F/Gas 9. Turn occasionally, and once brown, add the wine. Continue roasting at the same temperature for 1 hour, checking that the sauce is not burning. Add hot water if needed and stir from time to time. Place a sheet of foil tightly over the roasting pan and continue cooking in the same way for another hour. Remove from the oven, place on a chopping board and slice lengthways. Place the slices on a serving platter and keep hot. To make the sauce heat in a pan the olives, butter, pepper, and several tablespoons of the roasting juice. When the sauce is ready spread over the pork slices and serve hot.

Rabbit with Olives and Sausage
Coniglio con olive e salsiccia

Serves 4

1.5kg (3¼lb) rabbit, cut into 8 pieces
5 tablespoons extra virgin olive oil
2 pinches of salt
a handful of fresh rosemary and sage, crushed
200ml (7fl oz) lager
150g (5oz) sausages, skins removed
50g (2oz) green olives, stoned and chopped
freshly ground black pepper

Place the rabbit pieces, side by side, in a large casserole. Add the oil, salt and herbs, and brown over a high heat. Pour in 100ml (3½fl oz) of the lager and allow to evaporate. Cover, lower the heat and cook for 30 minutes. Stir from time to time, adding more lager if necessary to prevent the meat drying out. Remove the cover and add the sausages, crushing them with a wooden spoon. Add the olives and a good grind of pepper and stir. Replace the cover and continue cooking for another 30 minutes or more; the rabbit should be tender. During this final cooking phase, stir the rabbit pieces often to avoid burning and add more lager, a bit at a time. The rabbit should be very tasty, and can be served with polenta.

Rabbit with Olives and Walnuts
Coniglio con olive e noci

Serves 4–6

50ml (2fl oz) extra virgin olive oil
1 sprig of fresh rosemary
10 fresh sage leaves
2 bay leaves
1 fresh chilli, chopped
salt and freshly ground black pepper
80g (3oz) speck, finely chopped
30g (1oz) butter
80g (3oz) walnuts, finely chopped
50g (2oz) green olives, stoned and finely sliced
1.5kg (3¼lb) rabbit, cut into 8 pieces
300ml (½ pint) dry white wine

Heat the oil in a large casserole and add the herbs, chilli, 2 pinches of salt, the speck, butter and walnuts. Add the rabbit pieces and brown them without burning. Pour in 100ml (3½fl oz) of the wine and allow to evaporate, then lower the heat and add a little hot water. Cover and cook for about 40 minutes, stirring occasionally. Add the remaining wine and a little more hot water, and adjust the seasoning if necessary. Add the olives and continue cooking until the rabbit is tender.

Serve very hot, accompanied by a potato purée.

It takes just like chicken

Wilful Behaviour, pp. 227–231

These thoughts accompanied him home, but as he turned into the final flight of steps leading up to the apartment, he made a conscious effort to leave them on the stairway until the following morning took him back into the world of death.

This decision proved a wise one, for there would have been no room for the people who filled his thoughts at a table that already held not only his family but Sara Paganuzzi, Raffi's girlfriend, and Michela Fabris, a schoolfriend of Chiara's, come to spend the night.

Because Marco had caused him to miss his lunch, Brunetti felt justified in accepting a second portion of the spinach and ricotta crêpes* that Paola had made as a first course. (…)

As his hunger diminished, he found himself better able to pay attention to what was going on around him, as though tuning in to a radio station. 'I think he's wonderful,' Michela sighed, encouraging Brunetti to change stations and tune in to Sara, but listening was no easier on that channel, save that the object of her adoration was his only son.

It was Paola who saved him by bringing to the table an enormous frying pan filled with stewed rabbit with what looked to him, as she set it down in the centre of the table, like olives. 'And walnuts?' he asked, pointing to some small tan chunks that lay on the top.

'Yes,' Paola said, reaching for Michela's plate.

The girl passed it to her but asked, sounding rather nervous, 'Is that rabbit, Signora Brunetti?'

'No, it's chicken, Michela,' she said with an easy smile, placing a thigh on the girl's plate.

Chiara started to say something, but Brunetti surprised her into silence by reaching over to pick up her plate, which he passed to Paola. 'And what else is in it?' Brunetti asked.

'Oh, some celery for taste, and the usual spices.'

Passing the plate to Chiara, Brunetti asked Michela, 'What movie were you and Chiara talking about?'

As she told him, not forgetting to extol the charms of the young actor who held her in thrall, Brunetti ate his rabbit, smiling and nodding at Michela as he tried to determine whether Paola had put a bay leaf in, as well as rosemary. Raffi and Sara ate quietly, and Paola came back to the table with a platter of small roasted potatoes and zucchini cooked with thin slices of almonds. Michela turned to the two previous films which had catapulted her actor to stardom, and Brunetti served himself another piece of rabbit.

As she spoke, Michela ate her way through everything, pausing only when Paola slipped another spoonful of meat and gravy on to her plate, at which point she said, 'The chicken is delicious, Signora.'

Paola smiled her thanks.

After dinner, when Chiara and Michela were back in her room, giggling at a volume achievable only by teenage girls, Brunetti kept Paola company as she did the dishes. He sipped at nothing more than a drop of plum liquor while Paola slipped the dishes into the drying rack above the sink.

'Why wouldn't she eat rabbit?' he finally asked.

'Kids are like that. They don't like to eat animals they can be sentimental about,' Paola explained with every indication of sympathy for the idea.

'It doesn't stop Chiara from eating veal,' Brunetti said.

'Or lamb, for that matter,' Paola agreed.

'Then why wouldn't Michela want to eat rabbit?' Brunetti asked doggedly.

'Because a rabbit is cuddly and something every city child can see or touch, even if it's only in a pet shop. To touch the other ones you have to go to a farm, so they aren't really real.'

'You think that's why we don't eat dogs and cats?' Brunetti asked.

'Because we have them around all the time and they become our friends?'

'We don't eat snake, either,' Paola said.

'Yes, but that's because of Adam and Eve. Lots of people have no trouble eating them. The Chinese, for example.'

'And we eat eel,' she agreed. She came and stood beside him, reached down for his glass, and took a sip.

'Why did you lie to her?' he finally asked.

'Because she's a nice girl, and I didn't want her to have to eat something she didn't want to eat or to embarrass herself by saying she didn't want to eat it.'

'But it was delicious,' he insisted.

'If that was a compliment, thank you,' Paola said, handing him back the glass. 'Besides, she'll get over it, or she'll forget about it as she gets older.'

'And eat rabbit?'

'Probably.'

'I don't think I have much of a feeling for young girls,' he finally said.

'For which I suppose I should be very grateful,' she answered.

Von Clausewitz at Rialto

I'm a peaceful person. However, like many of my sort, I take a keen interest in observing the behavior – one might even say the tactics – of those people who are not. Human aggression, no matter how we attempt to suppress it, will slip from whatever restraint is placed upon it, and all high notions regarding human behaviour will crumble in the face of the desire to expand and possess. This was a reality well understood by Carl von Clausewitz, the Prussian general whose *On War* is one of the classic texts on the subject.

A book about food and cooking might seem an odd place for the General to make an appearance, were it not for my conviction that his text is much favoured by Venetian women of a certain age. Perhaps they turn to it when the last grandchild is born, or when they finally stop dyeing their hair, or simply when they decide that, since there are not many more years left, they would prefer to live the last ones in the manner of the lion and not the lamb. For what else could explain the remarkably astute tactics common to the old women who do their grocery shopping at the Rialto Market?

Von Clausewitz took Napoleon – audacious, aggressive, careless of human life – as his example when he wrote about warfare, which the Prussian viewed as an inseparable part of normal political life. Diplomacy and negotiation came first, von Clausewitz argued, and only when both failed was one obliged to resort to warfare: once begun, war was to be absolute and merciless. Ah, how very like the behaviour of the women in the midst of whom I have been doing my grocery shopping for decades, though most of them seem to have overlooked the General's remarks about diplomacy and negotiation.

Let us begin with von Clausewitz's definition of war: 'War therefore is an act of violence intended to compel our opponent to fulfil our will.' The overriding desire of the aggression displayed by the old women at Rialto is, indeed, to compel the opponent to fulfil her will, namely that she be served the instant she arrives, regardless of how many people are already in line. The opponent is any other customer, and the act of violence is usually committed not against those people but against the established rule of taking a turn in the order in which people arrive at the counter.

'The compulsory submission of the enemy to our will is the ultimate object.' In order to compel this submission, von Clausewitz continues, 'The number (of troops) will determine victory . . . only it must be sufficiently great to be a counterpoise to all the other cooperating circumstances.' Further, he believes that 'the greatest possible number of troops should be brought into action at the decisive point'.

Obviously, a small woman weighing between fifty and fifty-five kilos, standing perhaps 1.5 metres tall, is not likely to bring the greatest number of troops into action in front of the pecorino, is she? Thus she will be forced to fall back on 'cooperating circumstances', which in her case are the traditions deep rooted in Italian society regarding the deference and respect which must be given to old people, especially old women, and which, well she knows, weaken her opponents sufficiently to render them vulnerable to her attack. Rather than bring up the cavalry at a particular moment, rather than fling the Imperial Guard into a charge in one last attempt at victory, she will use the wily stratagems of Feigned Astonishment. Usually, it works.

This manoeuvre is a simple one and is almost always successful. Its genius lies in its obviousness: surely no person would so brazenly push past six others lined up at the cheese counter unless she had a legitimate reason to do so? Like most unexpected attacks, it must be launched with nonchalance to keep the manoeuvre from being detected for as long as possible. It is important, too, that at this early stage the attacking forces avoid all physical contact. She is, after all, a small person and so can insinuate herself between shoulders and hips, avoid knocking over other people's shopping bags, and arrive smack up against the counter, first in line.

Once she is in possession of the territory, she will allow one person to be served ahead of her, the better to tranquillize the opposing forces: 'Stratagem implies a concealed intention, and is therefore opposed to straightforward dealing.' Then, at the question from the cheese-seller, '*Chi tocca?*' she will shoot up her hand to indicate that she is next and begin to give her first order. Italians, trained to be respectful (especially to a woman the same age as their grandmothers), will remain mute. The merchant, no doubt long familiar with her tactic, has the option of questioning her assertion and thus losing her as a customer or of passively serving her – another 'cooperating circumstance'. Should it happen, however, that her claim is called into question, she will employ the tactic of Feigned Astonishment and ask, 'Oh, were you before me?'

Should her opponent be tempted to answer sharply, perhaps slip into irony or sarcasm, the old woman will summon her forces with breathtaking speed and launch the attack of Bold Denial. 'I didn't see you; I was here first; that man in the green shirt was the only one here when I got here; all I want is one thing.' Should a person be so rash as to ignore the centuries of training to which the Italians waiting at the counter have been subjected and be tempted to argue with her, that person risks going against von Clausewitz's admonition that 'even if we are decidedly superior in strength, and are able to repay the enemy his victory by a greater still, it is always better to forestall the conclusion of a disadvantageous combat'. Bear in mind that *any* opposition to one of these women constitutes a 'disadvantageous combat', for she will not retreat and she will never surrender: she was there first, and that is the end of it. They know, these old women, that 'there is nothing in War which is of greater importance than obedience', and in Italy people are still obedient to the social rule that dictates patience with the old. Further, most people doing the grocery shopping are women, and they are usually more obedient to social convention than are men.

Sometimes, however, it proves impossible for her to charge to the head of the queue, and she is constrained to call out her order from the flanks: in this case, she employs what the General calls 'those extraordinary mental powers required in a general', and resorts to Bold

Denial. Entrenched in her position, she waves off the existence of a queue, insisting that she was there first, indeed is quite exasperated at having been kept waiting so long.

The success of either of these tactics – see Book III, Chapter 7 for what the good General has to say about perseverance – allows for escalation, and she is thus free to begin giving her order, a feinting manoeuvre that distracts from the audacity of her invasion by diverting attention to the supposed poor quality of the merchandise. Inevitably, this will include comments about the prosciutto she bought last time, a fierce admonition that the fat be cut from the Speck before it is sliced, abrupt inquiries into the age of the ricotta, and a sharp exhalation of breath indicative of outraged disbelief at any assertion regarding the quality of the mozzarella.

Von Clausewitz understands not only war but the secrets of the human heart: 'Of all the noble feelings which fill the human heart in the exciting tumult of battle, none, we must admit, are so powerful and constant as are the soul's thirst for honour and renown.' Consider for a moment how little honor and renown are left to these women as they move towards the end of their lives; consider how shrunken are the battlefields where once, in their youth and their prime, they could do combat in search of respect and power. Strength gone, perhaps widowed or living alone, they are forced to use other means to obtain victory. Their 'concealed intention' – at least they believe it is concealed – is above all a return to their former status, to their former honour and renown.

Whether they are doing battle in front of the salami or cheese or defending their position in front of the fruit and vegetables, this desire to defend their honour will not leave them. They are the only clients – other than tourists, who simply don't know any better – who will dare to lay their hands on the peaches or rip their own bananas from the bunch.

In the course of four decades, both as a combatant and as a neutral observer when at Rialto with friends, I have never known one of these old women to surrender or retreat. Deaf to all protest, and in the face of comment, sarcasm, or abuse, they have all stood firm, facing the enemy head-on: they will have *this* melon and *these* grapes. As words are fired above them, they will pinch the apricots to see that they are firm, break off a leaf of basil to see – to see what? that it is not plastic? They will complain about the freshness of the zucchini, the size of the potatoes, the few tattered leaves on the outside of a head of lettuce. And, even as the glances and mutterings of the other customers burst like grenades above their heads, so fierce does their attack remain that most merchants will give in and strip off the offending leaves or reject a peach if its skin is rougher than that of a newborn baby's.

And how are we meant to respond, those of us standing in line as they subtly position themselves in front of us? '. . . for in such dangerous things as War, the errors which proceed from a spirit of benevolence are the worst'. Doomed by our own good will and sympathy, we commit these errors of benevolence, year after year, leaving the field of battle to these wrinkled Amazons. As they shove past us, we should bear in mind that these old women have no choice but to obey von Clausewitz's order that 'the victualling of the troops themselves comes first and must be done almost daily'. Themselves obedient to the rule of war, they have no choice but to attempt to banish all enemies and triumph on the field of battle.

And what of us, as we stand in line, in the fullness of our health and vigour? We might be well advised to recall that 'No battle can take place unless by mutual consent.' If we do persist in combat, what do we gain? Three minutes? Perhaps, then, it is better to leave the field of battle to our adversaries and let them be first in line, restored to honour and renown. Let them return to their tents carrying the laurel (or thyme, or parsley) of victory, at least for as long as it takes them to buy *due etti di mortadella e un po` di ricotta affumicata.*

Desserts · *Dolci*

Desserts are an experiment in alchemy. They are not suited to those who don't want to get fat. They are, however, ideally suited to those who want to be reconciled with their fellow man and the world around them. What could be more enticing on a cold, rainy day, for example, than to come home to a warm house and the aroma of apple cake?

We all have to admit that desserts are a great invention, but to make a success of them it is absolutely crucial to follow the recipes *to the letter*. Desserts are the only dish that place this obligation on us.

There are an infinite number of recipes, often stemming from ancient family traditions going back centuries. These recipes are the result of exhaustive experiments with varying quantities and blends – the eggs beaten in a certain way, the sugar added first rather than last, the addition of one aroma rather than another, or cornstarch rather than flour – that have put us on the map by giving us the perfect dessert: 'our' dessert.

Roberta Pianaro

DESSERTS
Dolci

Oven-baked apples with confectioner's custard and cream   250
Mele al forno con crema pasticcera e panna

Apple, lemon, orange and Grand Marnier cake   252
Torta di mele, limone, arancia, Grand Marnier

Almond cake   256
Torta di mandorle

Strawberry cake with cream   257
Torta di fragole con panna

Chocolate cake   258
Torta di cioccolato

Ricotta cake   259
Torta di ricotta

Pear cake with confectioner's custard   260
Torta di pere e crema pasticcera

Pears cooked in wine with yoghurt   264
Pere cotte al vino con yogurt

Fried cherries   265
Ciliegie fritte

OVEN-BAKED APPLES WITH CONFECTIONER'S CUSTARD AND CREAM
Mele al forno con crema pasticcera e panna

4 Golden Delicious apples
2 tablespoons sugar
2 pinches of powdered cinnamon
250ml (8fl oz) fresh cream

For the custard
3 medium egg yolks
150g (5oz) sugar
a pinch of salt
a packet of vanillin
50g (2oz) flour
a bit of lemon peel
500ml (18fl oz) milk

Peel and core the apples and cut in half. Arrange them in an ovenproof dish, sprinkle with the sugar and cinnamon, and place in a preheated oven at 240°C/475°F/Gas 9 for 20 minutes. Remove from the oven and leave to cool to room temperature.

Place the egg yolks in a bowl and beat them with the sugar until frothy. Add the salt, vanillin and flour, mix well and add the hot milk, a bit at a time. When the custard is smooth, pour into a non-stick pan, add the lemon zest and cook over moderate heat, stirring constantly. Once the custard has thickened, remove the lemon zest and continue cooking, stirring, for a few more minutes. While still hot, pour the custard over the apples to cover them. Place back in the hot oven, cook for a few minutes until the custard deepens in colour, then remove and cool. Whip the fresh cream until thick and spread over the top.

Delicious lukewarm or cold. Needs to be prepared in advance.

APPLE, LEMON, ORANGE AND GRAND MARNIER CAKE
Torta di mele, limone, arancia, Grand Marnier

150g (5oz) butter
150g (5oz) sugar
salt
2 medium eggs, beaten
150g (5oz) flour
1 teaspoon baking power
breadcrumbs
1kg (2¼lb) apples
juice of ½ a lemon
100ml (3½fl oz) Grand Marnier
60g (2½oz) candied orange peel, chopped

Place 100g (3½oz) of melted butter, 100g (3½oz) of sugar and a pinch of salt in a bowl and mix thoroughly. Add the eggs, continue stirring, and finally blend in the flour and baking powder. The resulting dough should be soft enough to be spread out on the bottom of a cake tin measuring 26cm (10 inches) in diameter. Butter and sprinkle with the breadcrumbs.

Peel the apples, cut them into thin slices and place them in another bowl. Splash with the lemon juice and add the remaining 50g (2oz) of sugar and the 50g (2oz) of melted butter. Mix well, adding the Grand Marnier and finally the candied orange peel. Pour over the dough and level out the surface. Place in a preheated oven and bake at 180°C/350°F/Gas 4 for at least 1 hour.

Paola's famous apple cake

A Sea of Troubles, pp.238–240

Paola went to the counter and removed the round top from the porcelain cake dish she had inherited from her Great-Aunt Ugolina in Parma. Inside it, as Brunetti had hardly dared hope, was her apple cake, the one with lemon juice and enough Grand Marnier to permeate the whole thing and linger on the tongue for ever.

'Your mother is a saint,' he said to the children.

'A saint,' repeated Raffi.

'A saint,' intoned Chiara as an investment towards a second helping.

After dinner, Brunetti took a bottle of Calvados, intent on maintaining the apple theme introduced by the cake, and went out on to the terrace. He set the bottle down, then went back into the kitchen for two glasses and, he hoped, his wife. When he suggested to Chiara that she do the dishes, she made no objection.

'Come on,' he said to Paola and returned to the terrace.

He poured the two glasses, sat, put his feet up on the railing, and looked off at the clouds drifting in the far distance. When Paola sat down in the other chair, he nodded towards the clouds and asked, 'You think it'll rain?'

'I hope so. I read today that there are fires in the mountains up above Belluno.'

'Arson?' he asked.

'Probably,' she answered. 'How else can they build on it?' It was a peculiarity of the law that undeveloped land upon which the construction of houses was forbidden lost that protection as soon as the trees on it ceased to exist. And what more efficient means of removing trees than fire?

Neither of them much wanted to follow up this subject, and so Brunetti asked, 'What's wrong?'

One of the things Brunetti had always loved about Paola was what he persisted, in the face of all her objections to the term, in thinking of as the masculinity of her mind, and so she did not bother to feign confusion. Instead, she said, 'I find your interest in Elettra strange. And I suppose if I were to think about it a bit longer, I'd probably find it offensive.'

It was Brunetti who echoed, innocently, 'Offensive?'

'Only if I thought about if much longer. At the moment, I find it only strange, worthy of comment, unusual.'

'Why?' he asked, setting his glass on the table and pouring some more Calvados.

She turned and looked at him, her face a study in open confusion. But she did not repeat his question; she attempted to answer it. 'Because you have thought about little except her for the last week, and because I assume your trip to Burano today had something to do with her.'

Other qualities he had always admired in Paola were the fact that she was not a snoop and that jealousy was not part of her makeup. 'Are you jealous?' he asked before he had time to think.

Her mouth dropped open and she stared at him with eyes that

might as well have been stuck out on stalks, so absolute was her attention. She turned away from him and said, addressing her remarks to the campanile of San Polo, 'He wants to know if I'm jealous.' When the campanile did not respond, she turned her eyes in the direction of San Marco.

As they sat, the silence lengthening between them, the tension of the scene drifted away as if the mere mention of the word 'jealousy' had sufficed to chase it off.

The half-hour struck, and Brunetti finally said, 'There's no need for it, you know, Paola. There's nothing I want from her.'

'You want her safety.'

'That's for her, not from her,' he insisted.

ALMOND CAKE
Torta di mandorle

6 medium egg whites
300g (11oz) sugar
300g (11oz) shelled almonds
a little butter for greasing the baking tin
breadcrumbs for sprinkling on the baking tin
icing sugar

Place the egg whites in a bowl and beat until they form stiff peaks. Gradually whisk in the sugar. Grind the almonds finely in a food processor and add to the egg and sugar mixture. Grease a springform baking tin (diameter 24cm/9.5 inches) with the butter, sprinkle with the breadcrumbs and pour in the mixture. Place in a hot oven and bake at 180°C/350°F/Gas 4 for 45 minutes. When cooled, sprinkle with icing sugar.

STRAWBERRY CAKE WITH CREAM
Torta di fragole con panna

800g (1¾lb) strawberries
6 medium eggs, separated
250g (9oz) sugar
200g (7oz) sponge-fingers, crumbled
butter and flour for the baking tin
250ml (8fl oz) fresh whipping cream

Wash and dry the strawberries, cut into small pieces and set aside. Beat the egg yolks with the sugar in a bowl until frothy. Add the carefully crushed ladyfingers and the strawberries, mixing thoroughly to obtain a homogeneous blend. In another bowl whip the egg whites until they form stiff peaks and fold gradually into the strawberry mixture. Pour into a buttered and floured springform baking tin, measuring 26cm (10 inches) in diameter. Place in a preheated oven and bake for at least 1 hour at 180°C/350°F/Gas 4. Whip the cream in a bowl until very firm. Keep in the refrigerator until the cake is ready to be served. The cake should be served when still warm, with the cold cream.

CHOCOLATE CAKE
Torta di cioccolato

200g (7oz) unsweetened dark chocolate
50g (2oz) butter
170g (6oz) sugar
4 medium eggs, separated
1 tablespoon flour
60g (2½oz) cornflour
1 package baking powder (baker's yeast)
butter and flour for the baking tin

In a small non-stick pan melt the chocolate with the butter and 4 tablespoons of water over low heat, stirring occasionally, making sure the chocolate doesn't burn. Pour the chocolate into a bowl and mix thoroughly with the sugar and egg yolks. Blend in the flour, cornflour and baking powder. Beat the egg whites until they form stiff peaks and fold into the mixture. Pour into a springform cake tin measuring 26cm (10 inches) in diameter and bake in a preheated oven at 180°C/350°F/ Gas 4 for 40 minutes.

This is a cake that can be filled with cream or jam.

Ricotta Cake
Torta di ricotta

5 medium eggs, separated
100g (3½oz) sugar
300g (11oz) compact ricotta cheese
100g (3½oz) shelled almonds, ground to a powder
50g (2oz) raisins, washed and pressed
50g (2oz) candied orange, chopped
a packet of vanillin
grated rind of 1 organic lemon
butter and breadcrumbs for the baking tin

In a mixing bowl beat the egg yolks with the sugar, using a whisk. Add the ricotta cheese and the ground almonds to form a smooth cream. Next add the raisins, candied orange, vanillin and lemon rind and continue to stir. Beat the egg whites until they form very stiff peaks and fold into the mixture. Blend well and pour into a buttered cake tin (24cm/9.5 inches diameter) sprinkled with the breadcrumbs. Place in a preheated oven and bake at 180°C/350°F/Gas 4 for 45 minutes.

PEAR CAKE WITH CONFECTIONER'S CUSTARD
Torta di pere e crema pasticcera

For the sponge cake
5 medium egg yolks
150g (5oz) sugar
juice of 1 lemon, strained
150g (5oz) potato flour
vanillin x 2
2 teaspoons baking powder
butter and flour for the baking tin
3 medium egg whites

For the pears
350g (12oz) Kaiser pear flesh, peeled and chopped
120g (4oz) sugar

For the custard
2 medium egg yolks
75g (2¾oz) sugar
25g (1oz) flour
a pinch of salt
half a small packet of vanillin
250ml (8fl oz) milk
a long piece of lemon zest
2 tablespoons Cointreau

Beat the egg yolks with the sugar until frothy using a whisk. Add the lemon juice, flour, one vanillin and baking powder and mix well. Finally, beat the egg whites, until stiff and fold into the mixture. Pour into a springform cake tin, buttered and floured, measuring 26cm (10 inches) in diameter. Place in a preheated oven and bake at 180ºC/350ºF/Gas 4 for 35 minutes.

Meanwhile, place the pears, sugar and 100ml (3½fl oz) of water in a non-stick pan and cook over moderate heat for about 30 minutes. The pears should be transparent and the sauce a syrup.

To make the custard, beat 2 egg yolks with the sugar in a bowl until frothy, using a whisk. Add the flour, salt and second vanillin and mix well. Heat the milk and gradually add to the mixture. Pour into a non-stick pan, add the lemon zest and cook over low heat, stirring often. After several minutes the custard will thicken, but continue cooking for another 5 minutes, watching to make sure it doesn't stick. When cooled, discard the lemon zest and stir in the Cointreau.

When the sponge cake, pears and custard are completely cooled, assemble the cake. Using a very long knife, cut the sponge cake into 3 thin discs, and place one carefully on a round cake plate. Spread over the pears and their syrup, setting some aside for the final garnish. Place the second disc on top, spreading with most of the custard. Add the third and last disc, and garnish it with the remaining custard and pears. Place the cake in the refrigerator and serve slightly chilled.

The perfect compliment to philosophy: pear cake with cream

Wilful Behaviour, pp. 291–293

At lunch that day, an unusually silent Brunetti listened as family talk swirled around him: Raffi said he needed a *telefonino*, which prompted Chiara to say that she needed one as well. When Paola demanded what either of them needed it for, both said it was to keep in touch with their friends or to use in case they were in danger.

When she heard this, Paola cupped her hands at the corners of her mouth, creating a megaphone, and called across the table to her daughter, 'Earth to Chiara. Earth to Chiara. Can you hear me? Come in, Chiara. Can you read me?'

'What's that mean, *Mamma*?' Chiara demanded, making no attempt to disguise her annoyance.

'It's to remind you that you live in Venice, which is probably the safest place in the world to live.' As Chiara started to object, Paola ran right over her: 'Which means that it is unlikely that you are going to be in danger here, aside from *acqua alta*, that is, and a *telefonino* isn't going to be much help against that.' And again, as Chiara opened her mouth, Paola concluded, 'Which means no.'

Raffi attempted to render himself as invisible as it was possible to be while eating a second piece of pear cake buried in whipped cream. He kept his eyes on his plate and moved slowly, like a gazelle attempting to drink from a pool it knew to be infested with crocodiles.

Paola did not strike, but she did float to the surface and peer at him with reptilian eyes. 'If you want to buy yourself one, Raffi, go ahead. But you pay for it.' He nodded.

Silence fell. Brunetti had been somewhere else during all of this or at least he had not been paying much attention to the scuffle, though

Paola's disapproval of what she considered their children's profligacy had caught his attention. With no preparation, he asked out loud, addressing them all equally, 'Aren't you ashamed that you pay all of your attention to acquiring as much money as you can, without giving any thought to truth and understanding and the perfection of your soul?'

Surprised, Paola asked, 'Where'd all that come from?'

'Plato,' Brunetti said and began to eat his cake.

The rest of the meal passed in silence, Chiara and Raffi exchanging inquisitive looks and shrugs, Paola trying to figure out the reason for Brunetti's remark or, more accurately, to understand which particular circumstances or actions had led him to recall the quotation, which she thought she recognized from the *Apology*.

Pears Cooked in Wine with Yoghurt
Pere cotte al vino con yogurt

Serves 4

4 Kaiser pears
150ml (¼ pint) Greek yoghurt
3 tablespoons sugar
a sprinkle of cinnamon
5 cloves
100ml (3½fl oz) fortified sweet white wine

Peel the pears and cut them in half lengthways. Remove the core, scooping out the surrounding bits in the centre. Place them side by side in a non-stick pan and sprinkle with the sugar and cinnamon. Add the cloves and the wine, then cover and cook over a high heat for 10 minutes. Remove the lid, lower the heat and reduce the sauce further for about 15 minutes. The pears should be transparent and slightly caramelized. Arrange them on a serving platter, placing a tablespoon of cold yoghurt in the centre of each. Always serve lukewarm.

These are delicious and can also be served with ice cream.

FRIED CHERRIES
Ciliegie fritte

Serves 4
500g (1lb 2oz) cherries, with their stems
2 medium eggs
6 tablespoons milk
a pinch of salt
2 tablespoons sugar
150g (5oz) flour
1 teaspoon baking powder
1 tablespoon extra virgin olive oil
icing sugar to garnish
lots of sunflower oil for frying

Wash the cherries and dry thoroughly. Beat the eggs with the milk, salt, sugar and flour. Add a tablespoon of oil to the baking powder and mix to obtain a smooth batter, not too runny, and add this to the mixture. Dip the cherries into the mixture, a few at a time, holding them by their stems. Once coated with the batter, plunge them into the hot oil (but not too hot, as this will burn the cherries). Once they're golden, place them on absorbent paper to dry and then stack on a plate. Sprinkle with icing sugar and serve at room temperature.

INDEX

273

DONNA LEON has lived in Venice for many years and previously lived in Switzerland, Saudi Arabia, Iran and China, where she worked as a teacher. Her previous novels featuring Commissario Brunetti have all been highly acclaimed; including *Friends in High Places*, which won the CWA Macallan Silver Dagger for Fiction, *Through A Glass, Darkly, Suffer the Little Children, The Girl of His Dreams,* and most recently, *About Face.*

ROBERTA PIANARO, born in 1948, has a jewellery workshop and a much used kitchen. Donna Leon calls Roberta the 'Risotto Queen' and often gets to enjoy her cooking. Just as well, for numerous dishes from Roberta's kitchen are served to the Brunettis as well.

TATJANA HAUPTMANN was born in Wiesbaden in 1950. After attending the Werkkunstschule in Offenbach, she worked as an apprentice graphics artist at the Werkkunstschule in Wiesbaden for three years, and for ZDF television afterwards.